A PICTORIAL HISTORY OF THE MOVIES

A PICTORIAL HISTORY OF THE
MOVIES

Mary Davies, Janice Anderson and Peter Arnold

DOMUS BOOKS

Originally published in Great Britain by
The Hamlyn Publishing Group Limited,
Astronaut House, Feltham, Middlesex, England

Copyright © 1975 The Hamlyn Publishing Group Limited

First published in the United States in 1976
by Domus Books
400 Anthony Trail, Northbrook, Illinois 60062

ISBN 0-89196-004-X

Library of Congress Catalog Card Number 76-7325

Filmset by Keyspools Limited, Golborne, Lancashire
Printed in Hong Kong by Leefung-Asco Printers Limited

Contents

The Beginnings

The Cinema to 1914

In the beginning, as all histories of the movies must start, there were the Lumière brothers. On 28 December 1895, Louis and Auguste Lumière showed a paying audience in Paris their *Cinématographe*, which projected moving film onto a large screen. The twentieth century's own art form, the motion picture, was born.

It had had a long gestation period. For many years, inventors had been trying to find ways to make pictures move, while as far back as the seventeenth century, the principle of the magic lantern – that a brightly lit object put in front of a magnifying lens will project its inverted image onto a screen in a darkened room – had been known in Europe. In the 1830s, the work of Fox Talbot in England and Daguerre in France led to the creation of photography. From then on, many men in Europe and the United States experimented with ways of making and projecting moving photographs.

By the 1880s Eastman had made his first roll-paper film for the Kodak cameras, and Thomas Alva Edison had taken his first steps towards the recording and reproduction of motion-pictures. The recorder he and his assistant, William Dickson, had developed by 1890 was the Kinetograph, which took rapid sequences of photographs. Then, in 1891, came their

above
Sarah Bernhardt's flamboyant stage acting style did not transfer well to the screen in Louis Mercanton's *La Reine Elisabeth* (1912).

left
Girls from the Folies Bergère frequently appeared in fantastic guise in the films of Georges Méliès.

right
Thomas Alva Edison's first film studio, used from 1894, was an extraordinary patched-together shed called 'The Black Maria'. By the time *How Bella Was Won* was made in 1911 Edison was just one of several big companies in operation, Vitagraph and Biograph having begun in 1897.

HOW BELLA WAS WON
FROM "OUR MUTUAL FRIEND" BY CHAS. DICKENS
A TALE WHICH HOLDETH CHILDREN
ROM PLAY AND OLD MEN FROM
THE CHIMNEY CORNER"
SIR PHILIP SIDNEY

reproduction system: the Kinetoscope,
which gave one viewer at a time a form
of peepshow.

It was the combining of the principle
of the Kinetoscope with that of the
magic lantern which made the cinema
possible, and the Lumière brothers
were the first to demonstrate publicly
how it could be done.

Within a year, the cinema had
spread throughout Europe and America. In a very short time it became
a huge commercial enterprise. The
first permanent film theatre was built

as early as 1897 (in France), and just ten years later in the United States there were about 10,000 'nickelodeons' in operation. In France, Leon Gaumont and Charles Pathé built up empires which were to spread throughout the world. Everywhere, public demand for films was so great that cinema owners very soon could not afford to buy their films, and began to rent them. The industry quickly established its familiar three-part set-up of producer, distributor and exhibitor.

In America, film companies – Edison, Vitagraph, Biograph and others – grew so quickly that by 1909 there was a fierce struggle for control of the industry in the East, which resulted in many smaller, independent companies, who were not part of the Motion Picture Patents Company, moving to California. By this time, too, the star system was developing, and public interest in the real actors and actresses behind the Company titles was being fostered by the first fan magazines.

Such an industry could not have been built on a mere toy or sideshow.

At first, film-makers were content to explore the possibilities of the new medium, developing techniques of camera movement – tracking, panning, long shot, medium shot, close-up, upside-down shots which could then be projected in reverse. Then, gradually, ideas of editing and of montage began to develop. Their effect was first noticeable in the work of the American Edwin S. Porter: *The Life of an American Fireman* (c. 1902) and *The Great Train Robbery* (1903). By 1905 the Englishman Cecil Hepworth was

showing a smooth editing technique in his film *Rescued by Rover*.

Finally, film-makers discovered that their toy could be – indeed, was – an art form. A Frenchman, Georges Méliès, led the way. Working from his earlier interests in the theatre and in magic, he made more than a thousand films before 1914, most of them playing marvellous and magic tricks with space and time, and creating a world of fantasy and wit far removed from the street scenes and trains coming into stations of many of his contemporaries in the cinema. The film which brought him international recognition was among his earliest: *A Trip to the Moon* (1902).

France was also responsible for the development of the 'film d'art' – prestige productions, often in costume, of historic or literary themes, and often starring famous theatre actors and actresses. They were a great influence on the film production of Italy, Russia, Britain and Denmark, and although they were often pretentiously overblown, they helped give the cinema an intellectual and social respectability.

The American film industry, with its huge home market, was from its beginnings strong enough not to fear European competition. The outbreak of the First World War in 1914 ensured that it, not the Europeans, would dominate world cinema.

The major force behind the rapidly maturing art of the cinema in America was David Wark Griffith. In his hundreds of films made before 1913, Griffith gradually extended the subject range of the cinema and the ways in which those subjects were expressed. His decision in 1911 to make his film of *Enoch Arden* a two-reeler instead of the usual one was greeted with misgiving by conservative exhibitors who were sure their audiences would not sit through anything so long. The spectacular success of the nine-reel, two-hour-long Italian epic *Quo Vadis?* in America in 1913 proved them wrong and set Griffith on a course which led to *The Birth of a Nation*.

Mack Sennett and Thomas Harper Ince, both of whom were first directors and then producers, were other major figures in the creation of the American film. Sennett's Keystone Studio was founded in 1912 and the comedies made there were a major factor in establishing America's world-wide commercial dominance of the film industry. Among the most momentous of Sennett's acts was his hiring of the 24-year-old Charlie Chaplin in 1913. Within a year, Chaplin was famous throughout the world.

Enrico Guazzoni's *Quo Vadis?* was a nation-wide success when it was shown in America in 1913.

opposite
Daniel, a Vitagraph film of 1913.

Horror and Fantasy

Dracula, Frankenstein and the freaks

Georges Méliès was the first to use fantasy in films. *The Lady Vanishes* (1896) explains itself. Other films had heads leaving bodies and the Devil turning into a priest, and *The Merry Frolics of Satan* (1907) contained 'fifty new tricks', none of which could prevent Méliès' bankruptcy, however. As his masterpiece, *A Trip to the Moon* (1902) was the first science-fiction film, Méliès is justly recognized as the pioneer of the fantasy film.

His lead was followed mainly in Germany. Paul Wegener was *The Student of Prague* (1913), whose lost shadow haunts him till he shoots it

and dies. Wegener co-directed and played *Der Golem* (1914), the first film of the legendary statue which comes to life. He followed up with *The Golem and the Dancing Girl* (1917) and in 1920 made *Der Golem* again, photographed by Karl Freund. Robert Wiene directed *The Cabinet of Dr Caligari* (1919), who is a hypnotist played by Werner Krauss. He exhibits at a fair an evil-looking Conrad Veidt, who commits murders while sleepwalking, but defies Caligari's instruction to murder a beautiful girl and abducts her instead, only to die while being chased. The distorted sets are

explained at the end when it is revealed that Caligari is the head of a lunatic asylum, and the whole story is a fantasy of one of his sick patients. F. W. Murnau made the first notable Dracula film, *Nosferatu* (1922) in which the Dracula figure is Count Orlok, played with claws and a skull-like face by Max Schreck. He scares the crew off a ship to Bremen, where his arrival starts a plague of death. The plucky heroine keeps him in her bedroom till dawn, when the sun's rays through the window dissolve him. Wiene directed Veidt again in *The Hands of Orlac* (1924), about a pianist

left
Werner Krauss as Dr Caligari, Conrad
Veidt as Cesare the somnambulist and
Lil Dagover as Jane in *The Cabinet of
Dr Caligari* (1919).

above
Metropolis (1926), the underground city
of workers leading lives like automatons.

right
Max Schreck as Count Orlok in
Nosferatu (1922), checking on the sun
which eventually destroyed him.

above
Bela Lugosi as *Dracula* (1931), carrying Helen Chandler into his crypt.

right
Lon Chaney as *The Phantom of the Opera* (1925) with his pupil and intended bride, Mary Philbin.

who loses his hands and has a murderer's grafted on in their place. The hands continue their deadly work despite Veidt, who is driven mad. A science-fiction fantasy set in the future, Fritz Lang's *Metropolis* (1926) is an underground city of suppressed workers, who are disturbed by a young girl preaching love and revolt. The evil Rotwang (Rudolf Klein-Rogge) abducts her and builds a robotrix in her image, but the revolt takes place and Rotwang is killed.

The era of German fantasy films ended with Murnau, Veidt, Freund, Lang and others going to Hollywood, where two very successful fantasy films had been made in 1925. A giant brontosaurus was the star of *The Lost World* and Lon Chaney, a make-up artist, was *The Phantom of the Opera*. A beautiful young singer is coached by an unseen voice, and sings at the Paris Opera House, which is terrorized by a murdering creature who lives in the sewers beneath. When the management reject her, a chandelier crashes into the audience, and the singer is led from the panic by her masked tutor,

through a labyrinth of tunnels to a subterranean bridal suite in a lakeside cavern. Realizing that her mentor and the Phantom are the same, she tears off his mask to reveal the skull-like face of Chaney. Audiences screamed.

A master of horror, Tod Browning, directed Chaney in *London After Midnight* (1927) where he is a vampire who prowls the ghostly night (in fact, he turns out to be a detective, disguised to catch a murderer). Chaney's make-up included wires in his eye-sockets, tightened before takes to

make his eyes bulge. The story of *The Cat and The Canary* (1927) has been repeated many times, often for laughs: the will of an eccentric millionaire is read at midnight in a haunted house, where the lovely heiress must stay to claim her inheritance. The Cat is an escaped criminal lunatic, and the girl awakes to find a claw reaching for her throat. Clocks, cobwebs and secret panels add to the chilly atmosphere.

The coming of sound added menace to the horror film, and Universal, who were making the genre their forte,

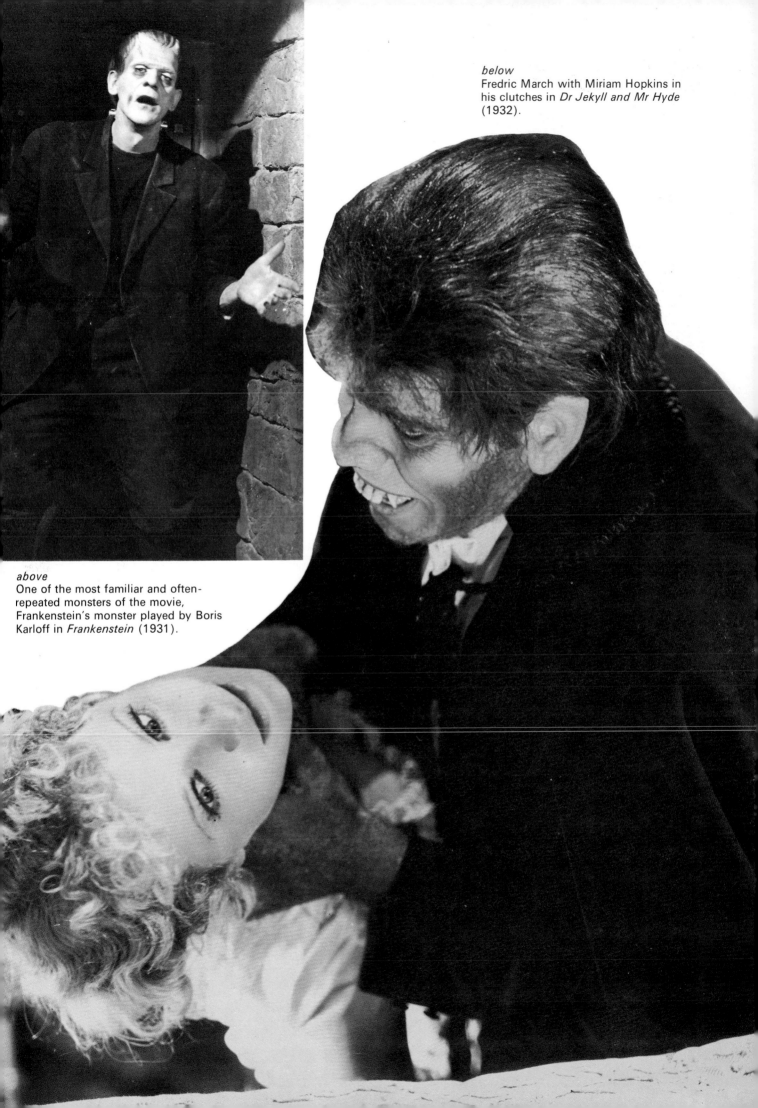

below
Fredric March with Miriam Hopkins in his clutches in *Dr Jekyll and Mr Hyde* (1932).

above
One of the most familiar and often-repeated monsters of the movie, Frankenstein's monster played by Boris Karloff in *Frankenstein* (1931).

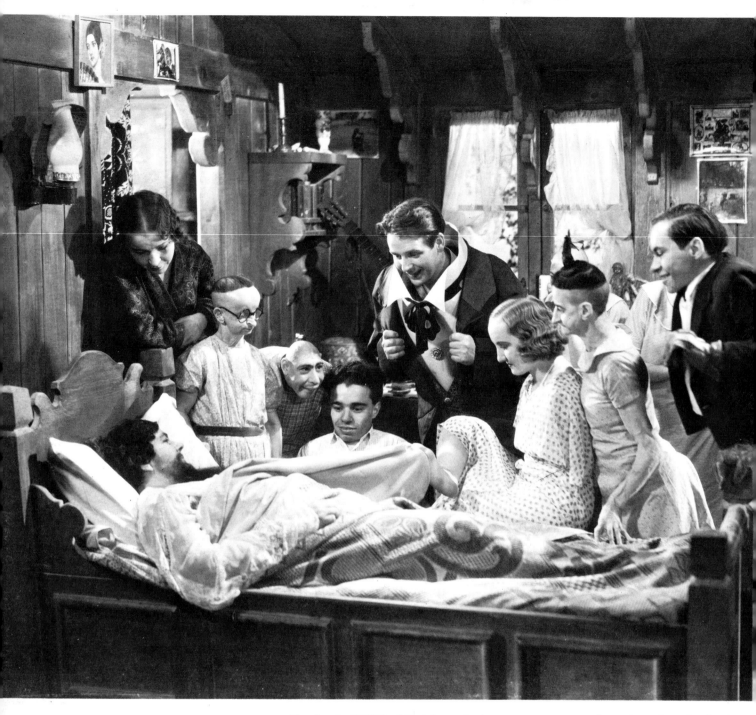

The *Freaks* (1932) of Tod Browning's film really were freaks who gave a circus trapeze artist a hen's body when she married and poisoned a midget for his money.

asked Tod Browning to direct *Dracula* (1931). Bela Lugosi gave the definitive performance, as his famous first words implied: 'I am Dracula'. He lives on blood, and assumes the shape of a bat to fly to the throats from which he drinks. Lugosi refused the part of the monster in Universal's next, *Franken-stein* (1931), previously filmed as a one-reeler (now lost) in 1910. Director James Whale chose Boris Karloff. Colin Clive played Dr Frankenstein, who builds a body from pieces of

corpses, not knowing that the brain his hunchback assistant has stolen is that of a killer. The shrouded body is given life by an electric storm, and the monster appears, complete with electrodes, flat head and heavy boots. Sensitive acting claims sympathy for him, and his death in a burning wind-mill, after killing his creator, has its sadness. The film has many sequels, only one, *The Bride of Frankenstein* (1935), surpassing the original. Karloff was again the monster, and James Whale directed what is regarded as his best work. The monster is dis-covered to have survived, after all, the burning windmill, and he be-friends Dr Pretorius (Ernest Thesiger) who gives an artificial brain to a fresh female corpse. In another, even more

violent, storm, the monster's bride is born. At the end of the film, when the monster is rejected by his bride, a tear rolls down his cheek, and saying 'We belong dead', he blows up the laboratory.

Horror flourished in 1932. Fredric March followed John Barrymore and others as *Dr Jekyll and Mr Hyde*, and won an Oscar for his transformation; Universal continued the gruesome work with *The Murders in the Rue Morgue*, with Lugosi as Dr Mirakle exhibiting a giant ape, who at night kidnaps girls as blood banks for Mirakle's experiments; Karloff was *The Mummy*, the first film directed by Karl Freund; and Tod Browning switched to MGM to direct *Freaks*, in which he used real freaks collected

from all over the world. The film was received with distaste, and was banned in Britain for 30 years, but some of Browning's best work is in it, and the final scene, where the freak's victim is turned into a human hen, is truly horrific.

All this activity was leading to the most famous fantasy film of all, *King Kong* (1933). King Kong was a monstrous gorilla (in fact he was a series of Willis O'Brien's rubber models), discovered on an African island, captured and brought to New York for exhibition. The monster escapes, devastates Manhattan, and carries Fay Wray, for whom he has developed a fondness, to the top of the Empire State Building. He is finally attacked by aeroplanes, and setting his queen

above left
Claude Rains as *The Invisible Man* (1933) wears bandages to give a visible cold shoulder to Gloria Stuart.

above right
The end of *King Kong* (1933). Fay Wray can be seen draped on a parapet of the Empire State Building.

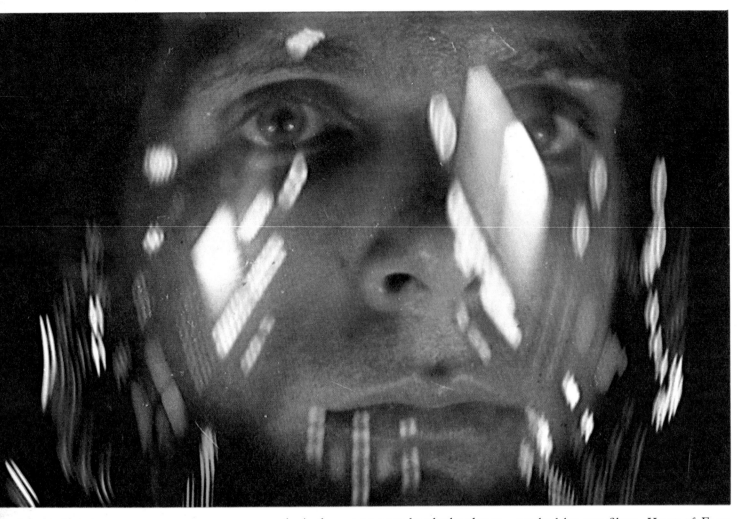

lovingly on a parapet, he plucks planes from the sky until their machine guns finally destroy him. The film is romantic fantasy rather than horror, and the sympathies of present-day audiences are entirely with the pathetic, puzzled gorilla.

There is no sympathy for *The Invisible Man* (1933), a technical triumph directed by James Whale, in which Claude Rains as the invisible man murders as a route to world power. More evil fantasy came from Tod Browning with *The Devil Doll* (1936). Dolls sold to his enemies by a fugitive from Devil's Island are really tiny people bent on murder and robbery. *The Thief of Baghdad* (1940) had fantasies more charming, such as a flying horse and a magic carpet.

In the 1940s Val Lewton produced and Jacques Tourneur directed a series of films with the emphasis on psychological fears which transformed the horror movie. The first was *The Cat People* (1942). Although women turn into fierce cats, the horror is less explicit than usual. The use of sounds and shadows enhances the fear, and the malignant presence of the cat is suggested rather than shown.

Traditional monsters were played out, and the end of their period was marked by two films, *House of Frankenstein* (1944) and *House of Dracula* (1945), in both of which Universal packed Frankenstein's monster, Dracula, the wolf-man and others. Soon (ultimate horror), Abbott and Costello were meeting them all. A fine post-script to the era was Peter Bogdanovich's *Targets* (1968) in which Karloff, musing over the golden age of fantasy, gets involved in modern horror with a teenage sniper.

Science fiction provided the next impetus to the genre. From 'another world' came *The Thing* (1951), a hairless flying vegetable, which drank human blood. Michael Rennie was a benevolent spaceman in *The Day the Earth Stood Still* (1951), sent with his robot to bring peace on earth. He failed. *The War of the Worlds* (1953) was based on H. G. Wells' story of a Martian invasion, in which the invaders were finally routed by common cold germs. *The Beast From 20,000 Fathoms* (1958) wreaked destruction after an atomic explosion woke it from its deep freeze sleep. Other monsters were soon appearing from the ocean floor to collect box office receipts. *Them!* (1953) were giant ants enlarged by atomic fall-out in the New Mexican desert. Japan entered the act with

Godzilla, King of the Monsters (1955), a dragon-like beast who dwarfed cities. *The Incredible Shrinking Man* (1957) was a variation on *The Devil Doll*, brought up-to-date by having the victim's troubles caused by radio-active dust. He was chased by a cat and battled with a spider. *The Village of the Damned* (1960) was visited by a force which caused its women to give birth to strange emotionless super-intellectual children with power to influence the minds of adults. The story was by John Wyndham, who also wrote *The Day of the Triffids* (1962), multiplying plants who destroyed everything in their path. Salt water killed them. Jean-Luc Godard's

Alphaville (1965) is a city whose inhabitants are ruled by a computer, which eliminates emotion from their lives (shades of *Metropolis*). The computer is defeated when fed indigestible poetry. *Barbarella* (1968) was Jane Fonda playing the comic-strip heroine in a science-fiction adventure and *2001 : A Space Odyssey* (1968), directed by Stanley Kubrick, was a space-travel horror movie. The film is full of powerful computers and other sophisticated machinery, and the humans of 2001 are robot-like caretakers of machines.

The old monsters made a comeback with Hammer Films, a British company which had a tremendous

above
Grant Williams, *The Incredible Shrinking Man* (1957), has foolishly left the doll's house to discover it's no fun being a mouse.

right
Janette Scott finds her barricades too weak to keep out a triffid in *The Day of the Triffids* (1962).

success with *The Curse of Frankenstein*
(1957). Hammer subsequently revived
all the monsters – Dracula, vampires,
were-wolves, the mummy – in glorious
colour, and were not averse to showing
blood, or even a bloody hatchet stuck
in a girl's head. Hammer made Peter
Cushing and Christopher Lee stars.

But the modern demon king was
not to be dislodged. Vincent Price
built a reputation for creepiness with
the help of a series of films directed by
Roger Corman, and loosely based on
Edgar Allen Poe stories, among them
The House of Usher (1960), *The Pit
and the Pendulum* (1961), *The Raven*
(1963) and *The Tomb of Ligeia* (1964).
Price has an air of superiority and

conceit, and a caressing assertive voice,
which convey menace superbly.

The Hammer and Price films purvey
horror tinged with amusement. The
shock is meant to be outrageous and
entertaining. Real horror in current
films uses psychological weapons: perhaps a dreadful event disturbs an
ordinary setting or story, upsetting
values carefully imposed by the director; or tension arises from the gradual
manifestation of evil from an un-
expected quarter.

In *The Fiends* (1955), a plot to
cause a fatal shock to a woman with a
weak heart leads to a supreme moment
of horror, when a fully-clothed and
staring-eyed 'corpse' submerged in a

bath slowly sits up. Hitchcock's *Psycho* (1960) has the heroine horrifyingly murdered in a shower, with blood swirling away down the plug-hole with the water. Having absorbed the surprise of the star being killed early in the picture, the audience is shocked again by the discovery that the chief suspect, Anthony Perkin's mother, is long dead and mummified.

A more subtle horror was evinced in *The Innocents* (1961), two children discovered by their frustrated governess to be possessed by ghosts. Or do the ghosts exist only in her imagination? The death of one child and the anguish of the governess are real enough.

In *The Birds* (1963), the routine life of Bodega Bay is suddenly disrupted by a concerted and inexplicable attack by massed birds who crash into buildings in great numbers in attempts to reach the people inside. Hitchcock

Anthony Perkins in *Psycho* (1960), with his rickety house in which he keeps the mummified body of his mother.

above
Catherine Deneuve staring at the remains of a rabbit which remind her of a foetus in *Repulsion* (1965).

left
Jessica Tandy, Tippi Hedren and Veronica Cartwright try to protect each other from *The Birds* (1963), Hitchcock's film of Daphne du Maurier's story.

knows that to some people birds share an atavistic menace with spiders, that their fragility curiously adds an eeriness to their attack, and that their uncharacteristic aggression, being motiveless, stirs deep discomfort.

An impotent pools-winning butterfly collector, Terence Stamp, kidnapped Samantha Eggar in *The Collector* (1965), and kept her in a cellar. His motive was to add a jewel to his collection, and glimpses of insanity as he attempts to woo her increase her claustrophobic terror.

There is claustrophobia, too, in Roman Polański's *Repulsion* (1965). The mind of a girl left alone in a flat begins to disintegrate. She has rape fantasies and hallucinations. Walls

crumble or grow soft and hands reach through them. Wandering about in her nightgown she kills her visiting boy-friend, and slashes her landlord to death with a razor. Catherine Deneuve plays the girl, who at the end is found lying under her bed amid a shambles of horror.

Rosemary's Baby (1968) was the result of rape by the Devil. Polański's film dealt with witchcraft and black magic, the dark corners of which offer limitless themes for modern horror. *The Exorcist* (1973) provided a surfeit which sickened, thus blunting its effect, but its publicity was in the tradition of horror films through the ages. The weak-hearted were warned to stay away.

opposite
Not a long-serving organist at the old-time picture palace, but Vincent Price wearing a mask of death as *The Abominable Dr Phibes* (1971).

above
Hammer beauty and the beast. David Prowse as the bloody beast and Madeleine Smith as the beauty in *Frankenstein and the Monster from Hell* (1974).

The Epic

Lions, tigers and a cast of thousands

The commercial cinema had not been in existence very long before film-makers realized that they had in their hand the power to re-create history, to re-live epic battles, rebuild the pyramids of Egypt, part the Red Sea, or engulf Pompeii in volcanic ash all over again. Sometimes, they have done so with an amazing vulgarity of style, a terrible – but often hilarious – jangling of anachronisms, and an insultingly low assessment of the intelligence of their audiences. But the best epics have been the work of men imbued with the power to create spectacle of breath-taking splendour in films of awesome conception.

Perhaps not surprisingly, the Italians were the first to make epics. With the ruins of Ancient Rome and Pompeii to inspire them, Italian film-makers looked to historical spectacle for their inspiration from the time they began making feature films. Arturo Ambrosio won international acclaim with the first of many versions of *The Last Days of Pompeii* in 1908, and Enrico Guazzoni's *Quo Vadis?* (1912) achieved the splendour of a showing before King George V in London and a society première in New York. Despite its long list of epic delights, including the soon-to-be obligatory cast of thousands, a large number of lions and horses, and huge sets designed by Guazzoni himself, this *Quo Vadis?* was very static, and it took Giovanni Pastrone with *Cabiria* (1913), a story of the Punic Wars, to show the real potential of the epic form. Pastrone allowed his camera to move; his audience, instead of sitting in the stalls watching events passing across the screen as if on stage, went with the camera through palaces, into temples, across landscapes.

In America, D. W. Griffith went further and changed the shape of the movie screen from nearly square to a much more vertical shape to allow room for his great vistas of ancient temples and palaces. It was the Italian epic which inspired him to move from the small-scale, intimate viewpoint which characterized most of the hundreds of films he had made for Biograph to think big. All the techniques of editing, lighting and composition which Griffith had developed in these

opposite
Sherman's march to the sea in Griffith's *The Birth of a Nation* (1915).

above
The high point of early Italian cinema: Giovanni Pastrone's *Cabiria* (1913).

right
Cecil B. DeMille's first version of *The Ten Commandments* (1923).

films, and which made him one of the greatest innovators in the history of the movies, were allied to his splendid new vision of the cinema to create the first true epics.

After trying out the form in *Judith of Bethulia* (1913), Griffith made *The Birth of a Nation* (1915), which told the story of the American Civil War. His next film, *Intolerance* (1916), sub-titled 'Love's Struggle Through the Ages', looked at intolerance in four periods of history (Modern America, Judea in AD 27, sixteenth-century France, and Babylon). The film set standards of authenticity and moral purpose which no epic made since has bettered and which few have matched.

The Bible

The Bible has been the inspiration for many of the best epics. Hundreds of films have been based on stories from both Testaments, most of them involving some sort of spectacle, and some reaching epic proportions. A certain inhibition about depicting the figure of Christ meant that the main character in New Testament films until quite recently was often a misty figure, or even just a hand, or a voice, or just a reflection in the faces of onlookers. Such was the great Cecil B. DeMille's reverence for his subject, that he would not allow the actors playing Christ and his Disciples in his *King of Kings* (1927) to drink or swear on set.

Little such reverence has stood in the way of the creators of Old Testament epics. DeMille's approach to the Old Testament, via two versions of *The Ten Commandments* (1923 and 1956), *The Sign of the Cross* (1932) and *Samson and Delilah* (1949), was on the grand scale. Most of his characters were cardboard, his lapses of taste

legion, and his interpretation of such concepts as 'decorum' and 'modesty' questionable. But his films have the style and vigour born of super-confidence and remain splendid entertainment.

Among the films telling the stories of biblical figures like Ruth, Solomon and Sheba, Salome, David and Bathsheba, and Barabbas, or attempting to cover large sections of the Bible, like George Stevens' *The Greatest Story Ever Told* (1964), Dino de Laurentiis' production of *The Bible* (1966) stands out not so much for its epic qualities – it was in fact rather dull – as for the stupendous thinking behind it. De Laurentiis wanted to make a nine-hour epic covering the first six books of the Old Testament, each book to be handled by a leading director: Welles, Fellini, or Bergman. In the end, John Huston directed the film, which covered only Genesis. The biblical epic to end all epics has still to find its maker.

The Epic Hero

The archetypal epic hero or heroine must be heroic, showing qualities of strength, endurance, beauty or power not given to ordinary mortals. Until David Lean's *Bridge on the River Kwai* (1957) and *Lawrence of Arabia* (1962), both of which featured heroes who were passive, thinking men forced into reluctant action, the epic had no room for the anti-hero. Everything must be in sharp black and white, and if the heroes or heroines of epics must die, they must do it with grandeur. There is probably no more splendid image in the epic genre than the last ride of El Cid – Charlton Heston as the dead Cid, bound upright in his horse's saddle, galloping from our sight into glorious legend. It is a heart-stopping moment.

The heroes of epics have come from legend – Helen of Troy, Robin Hood, Hercules, or El Cid – and from history. Napoleon, the young General, was the hero of Abel Gance's *Napoléon* (1927), and Napoleon, Emperor of the French, was the dominating character in two versions of *War and Peace* – King Vidor's splendid 1956 version, and the Russian Sergei Bondarchuk's seven-and-a-half-hours-long reconstruction of Tolstoy's novel made between 1963 and 1967 – as well as the 1970 USSR/Italy co-production *Waterloo*. Ivan the Terrible, Alexander the Great, Julius Caesar, Cromwell, General George Patton, and Winston Churchill have all been the subjects of films of epic proportions. Cleopatra, Queen of Egypt, Serpent of the Nile, has inspired more films than most. From Méliès in the 1890s to the *Carry On* team in the 1960s, Cleopatra has been a fascinating heroine.

above left
Theda Bara played *Cleopatra* in 1917.

left
Claudette Colbert was Cleopatra to Warren Williams' Caesar in DeMille's *Cleopatra* (1934).

above right
Vivien Leigh as Cleopatra and Claude Rains as Julius Caesar in Gabriel Pascal's extravagant *Caesar and Cleopatra* (1945).

right
Joseph L. Mankiewicz's *Cleopatra* (1963) starred Elizabeth Taylor as the Queen of Egypt.

Nero (Peter Ustinov) makes music while Rome burns in *Quo Vadis?* (1952). Leo Genn (*left*) played Petronius. On the right is Ralph Truman.

The Fall of Rome

The Bible and the lives of great men have been two major sources of the epic film. A third has been the crumbling of civilizations, the death-throes of empires. It is the drama of the subject, rather than the spectacular visual effects achieved, which gives such strength to films like Eisenstein's *October*, or to the many films about Ancient Rome.

The Roman Empire has inspired so many epics because its story has a two-fold theme: the crumbling of an empire contrasted with the rise of a new world religion, Christianity. It is a theme which has inspired some of the best epics, notably the two versions of *Ben Hur*, the silent version of 1926, starring Ramon Novarro and Francis X. Bushman, and William Wyler's 1959 CinemaScope version which starred Charlton Heston, as well as the several versions of *Quo Vadis?*, De-Mille's *The Sign of the Cross* (1932), the many re-makes of *The Last Days of Pompeii*, *The Robe* (1953), *Spartacus* (1960), and *The Fall of the Roman Empire* (1964).

top
The spectacular chariot race in William Wyler's version of *Ben Hur* (1959).

above
Ernest B. Schoedsack's 1935 version of *The Last Days of Pompeii*.

35

Epic Battles

Epic films have given the film-goer some of his most exciting moments when they have been re-creating battles. Among the great war scenes, the battle on the ice in Eisenstein's *Alexander Nevsky*, the cavalry charges in the Polish *The Knights of the Teutonic Order* (1960, directed by Aleksander Ford), or the whistle of the arrows at Agincourt in Olivier's *Henry V*, have pride of place.

As war has dominated the history of the twentieth century, so it has been a major theme of epics about the twentieth century. Not all of them have needed huge, expensive battle scenes to make their point: King Vidor's *The Big Parade* (1925) had its important battle scenes, but its greatest effect was achieved through its concentration on incidents in the lives of ordinary soldiers. But in some of them, the battles have been spectacular indeed: the storming of the Normandy beaches in *The Longest Day* (1962), the tank battles in the desert in *Patton: Lust for Glory* (1969) (even if, as the experts were quick to point out, they were the wrong tanks), the camel cavalry charges in *Lawrence of Arabia* (1962), or the re-creation of the aerial dog-fights in *The Battle of Britain* (1969).

above left
The Knights of the Teutonic Order (1960).

above right
Nevsky challenges the Grand Master of the Teutonic Order to single combat: the famous battle on the ice sequence from Eisenstein's *Alexander Nevsky* (1938).

Comedy

Chaplin's tramp to Tati's uncle

The Lumière brothers and Méliès made comedies before 1900. One of Méliès' 'moving picture shows' has a boy step on a gardener's hose. When the gardener examines the nozzle he gets a faceful of water. The dominance of France in the early days of cinema led to a French actor, Max Linder, becoming the first great screen comic. An elegant man picking his way through accident and disorder, he invented many of the much-repeated visual gags, using great observation to express the humour of such routine comedy as the drunk staggering home.

The American slapstick school was begun by Mack Sennett, of Irish descent, who set up the Keystone Film Company in 1912, and in the next three or four years produced, with the help of most of the great silent comics, hundreds of hilarious shorts. Keystone comedies needed plots only as framework for a rapid succession of gags: with actors getting pies in the face, falling into lakes and out of windows, escaping burning and crashing buildings and avoiding the cops and heavies. A great favourite was the comic chase, with the Keystone Cops and their quarry clinging precariously to cars which dodge at speed through hair-raising encounters with traffic, pedestrians, buildings and anything else which could be put in their way. Sennett's stars were Chaplin, Chester Conklin, cross-eyed Ben Turpin, Mabel Normand, the first great screen comedienne, and Roscoe 'Fatty' Arbuckle, whose name is still a byword for obesity.

The greatest of these was Charlie Chaplin, brought up in English music-hall. His first film was with Keystone, *Making a Living* (1914). Thirty-two films later (and still in 1914!) Chaplin had a major success with *Tillie's Punctured Romance*, a marathon of six reels. His pathetic and comic tramp figure was fully developed in *The Tramp* (1915), and was the basis of his future fame and fortune. He soon wrote and directed his own pictures, often daring: to make *Shoulder Arms* (1918), a parody on war when the tragedy of real war was fresh, seemed lunacy, but the film was a great success. In *The Gold Rush* (1925), Chaplin entertains in his imagination his New Year's Eve guests with a clever table top dance with rolls – but the guests do not arrive. He is forgotten. Not so

above left
The Keystone Cops set off on a chase. The car is only just beginning to pick up speed and they're nearly all on.

38

O A MILLION

a Paramount Picture

A lobby card for *If I Had a Million*
(1932), in which W. C. Fields and
Alison Skipworth drove around followed
by spare cars: dent one, take the next.

the scene, which is very funny and
intensely sad, the essence of Chaplin.
City Lights (1931) attacked capitalism
and the rich, *Modern Times* (1936)
attacked the machine age. In *The Great
Dictator* (1940) Chaplin caricatured
Hitler masterfully. His last great film,
Monsieur Verdoux (1947), is a comedy
based on Landru, the mass-murderer,
whose crimes, it is suggested, are no
worse than war. The film was banned
in some American states and failed,
but Chaplin thinks it is his most
brilliant film.

Like Chaplin, Buster Keaton came
from vaudeville, and shaped his own
material. He was the master of the
trick shot (some of those in *The Play-
house* (1921) are still not explained)
and the acrobatic. Two sequences
could serve to sum up his comic
genius. In *The Three Ages* (1923), he
escapes from a police station by
climbing on the roof, jumps across to
an adjoining building, falls several
storeys before grabbing a drainpipe,
which breaks away and crashes him
through a window into a fire station,
slides down the pole on to a departing
fire-engine which takes him to the
fire – back at the police station. In
Steamboat Bill Jr (1927), he fights a
cyclone, and the side of a multi-
storey house collapses on him – he
happens to be standing looking the
wrong way, exactly where a paneless
window falls, leaving him painless.
His masterpieces were *The Navigator*
(1924), adrift on a liner with his girl,
and having fun with its mechanics,
and *The General* (1927), a Civil War
comedy with a great train chase.
Because he rarely smiled, he was
called the 'Great Stone Face': in fact,
his face was extremely expressive.

The third great silent clown was Harold Lloyd, Keaton's equal in extricating himself from incredible predicaments. His character was a bespectacled, eager, shy, all-American boy, who often blundered into difficult situations and frequently ended by being chased. He is best remembered for his perilous balancing acts on skyscrapers: skipping from dislodged scaffold planks, clinging to parapets, or in *Safety Last* (1923) hanging from the arm of a clock.

Harry Langdon had a peculiar charm of his own. Baby-faced, he wandered baby-like and alone through an adult world, always being knocked down and picked up, curious and baffled.

Vaudeville comedians continued to flourish when sound came. Stan Laurel and Oliver Hardy had been successful in the last days of the silents; although their greatness came with talkies their technique was essentially of the silent era. They were a perfect pair, and

their comedy grew as their characters, reactions and catch-phrases became known: Stan scratching his head in confusion or crying, and Ollie complaining of 'another fine mess you've gotten me into', or raising his eyebrows at the camera as if to ask the audience's opinion of Stan's lunacy. They pioneered the 'tit-for-tat' gag, at its best in *Big Business* (1929), where James Finlayson breaks Ollie's watch, Ollie smashes his front door in retaliation and mayhem ensues as the trio troop from Finlayson's house to Stan and Ollie's car and back, carefully wrecking both, piece-by-piece, in a curiously logical 'your turn – my turn' manner, before a wondering crowd of onlookers.

Sound considerably helped W. C. Fields and the Marx Brothers, who mixed wise-cracks with visual gags. Of the Marx Brothers, lascivious Harpo didn't speak, Chico was always plotting and Groucho, with his aspirations to respectability, was full of

above
Harold Lloyd during one of his daredevil climbs around skyscrapers in *Safety Last* (1923).

top right
Charlie Chaplin in *Shoulder Arms* (1918), the second feature he made for the Essanay Studio, a brilliant comedy with a war theme.

right
Laurel and Hardy in *Men of War* (1929) exasperate James Finlayson, one of their regular protagonists, with a routine designed to get four sodas with only 15 cents.

ROAD T

repartee, sometimes of a suggestive kind. Their butt was usually the indomitable Margaret Dumont, often courted with ulterior motives by Groucho. When she tells him 'You'll find some pretty girl to go off with and leave me', he replies 'I'll send you a postcard'. Fields was a vaudeville juggler, whose film character was often a con-man, arrogant, mean and conceited; his well-known remark 'Any man who hates small dogs and children can't be all bad' sums him up well. Yet he was strangely sympathetic, fighting his battles with wives and authority with muttered thrown-away asides.

Eddie Cantor was funny with his big eyes, Jimmy Durante with his big nose, Joe E. Brown with his big mouth, Mae West with her ample proportions and earthy attitude to sex. When a hat-check girl says to her 'Goodness, what beautiful diamonds', she points out 'Goodness had nothing to do with it, dearie'. She also told the world 'It's not the men in my life

that count, it's the life in my men'. Two of her titles sum her up: *Diamond Lil* (1932) and *I'm No Angel* (1933), but she was more than a dumb blonde. She wrote much of her own material.

The wise-crack was most exploited by Bob Hope, who with Bing Crosby and Dorothy Lamour made a series of 'Road' films. Hope is the avaricious, cowardly, conceited funny-man, but his reputation is higher than his skill as a film comic. His cracks are often in-jokes about Paramount or Crosby's money. Abbott and Costello, too, enjoyed a fame which, compared with their films, is inexplicable. Danny Kaye was funnier with some frenetic patter and songs.

Film comedy in the 1930s and 1940s became less a matter of stars than of directors. Frank Capra presented a polished view of America in *It Happened One Night* (1934), a milestone in comedy. Claudette Colbert was a runaway heiress pursued by reporter Clark Gable (both won Oscars). They are forced to behave as if married (but

above left
Tom Ewell, infatuated by Marilyn Monroe's bravura performance of 'Chopsticks' in *The Seven Year Itch* (1955), leaned too close, and both slid to the floor.

BING CROSBY
BOB HOPE
DOROTHY LAMOUR

A PARAMOUNT PICTURE

MOROCCO

with
ANTHONY QUINN
DONA DRAKE
Directed by DAVID BUTLER
Original Screen Play by Frank Butler and Don Hartman

A lobby card for the third 'Road' taken
by Hope (*left*), Lamour and Crosby,
Road to Morocco (1942).

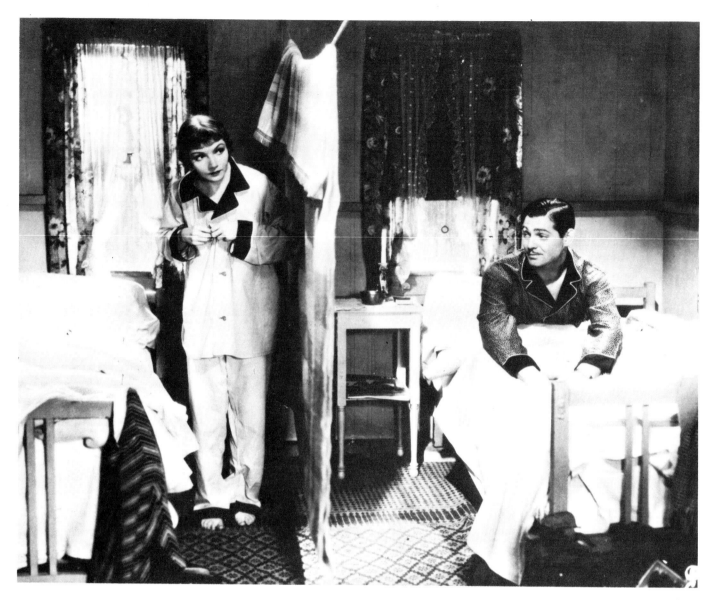

are obliged to have a screen separate their beds). The sophisticated treatment of risqué situations was immediately successful and Capra followed up with *Mr Deeds Goes to Town* (1936), where Gary Cooper inherits a fortune and resists everybody's attempts to get a slice. Ernst Lubitsch made refined comedies like *Trouble in Para-*

above
Claudette Colbert and Clark Gable won Oscars for *It Happened One Night* (1934), but Gable won no medals from vest manufacturers. When it was seen he didn't wear one, sales slumped.

opposite top
Louis Calhern, Spring Byington and Charles Coburn in Ernst Lubitsch's elegant comedy *Heaven Can Wait* (1943).

opposite bottom
The Philadelphia Story (1940), Cukor's comedy of the behaviour of the sophisticated rich, was remade as the musical *High Society* (1956). John Howard, Cary Grant, Katharine Hepburn and James Stewart in the original.

dise (1932), in which Herbert Marshall, a gentleman thief, woos Kay Francis, a lady thief. They steal from each other before attempting together to rob Miriam Hopkins. This film, and the later *Heaven Can Wait* (1943), where Don Ameche, dead, is sent back to earth by the Devil, is full of witty banter and charm. Between these films Lubitsch directed Garbo in *Ninotchka* (1939). The publicity said 'Garbo laughs', and so did the audiences. George Cukor directed *Dinner at Eight* (1933), full of good situations and lines, such as Marie Dressler's reply to Jean Harlow's 'I read that machinery is going to take the place of every profession' – 'My dear that's something *you* need never worry about.' Cukor made the witty *The Philadelphia Story* (1940), in which Katharine Hepburn starred, and directed Hepburn again with Spencer Tracy in *Adam's Rib* (1949), as husband-and-wife lawyers on opposite sides who exchange some sharp dialogue. Judy Holliday did well in this film, and Cukor starred her in

Born Yesterday (1950), and she proved the best of modern comediennes. The scene in which she upsets Broderick Crawford by beating him at gin rummy singing an inane song the while, is a delight. Other directors with a penchant for wit were Preston Sturges, principally with *The Lady Eve* (1941), Howard Hawks with *Bringing up Baby* (1938), which had Katharine Hepburn smoothly pursuing absent-minded Cary Grant (Baby was a leopard), and W. S. Van Dyke, whose *The Thin Man* (1934) showed a highly sophisticated couple, William Powell and Myrna Loy, enjoying their marriage and each other's weaknesses with style.

Billy Wilder has directed first-class comedies for many years. George Axelrod wrote the script for Wilder's *The Seven-Year Itch* (1955), as he did for Judy Holliday's *Phffft* (1954) and Audrey Hepburn's *Breakfast At Tiffany's* (1961). In *The Seven-Year Itch*, Tom Ewell, as a middle-aged married man cooped up alone in his apartment in a heat-wave, meets and has fantasies about Marilyn Monroe, the blonde upstairs. It is full of lovely touches, such as Monroe keeping her undies in the fridge, and the finally innocent encounter is played by both actors with considerable charm. Wilder also directed Monroe in *Some Like It Hot* (1959), in which she is in a female

Doris Day and Rock Hudson in *Send Me No Flowers* (1964), one of a series of several battle-of-the-sexes comedies Day made with Hudson, James Garner and Rod Taylor.

right
Jack Lemmon and Tony Curtis as fake girls and Marilyn Monroe as the triumphantly authentic article in *Some Like It Hot* (1959).

O.P.105

Will Hay (*left*) in *Oh, Mr Porter!* (1937), with his colleagues and rivals in low cunning, Moore Marriott and Graham Moffatt.

band with Jack Lemmon and Tony Curtis, impersonating girls to escape a band of criminals. Lemmon was in Wilder's *The Apartment* (1960), which he loans to executives of his company for amorous games only to fall for Shirley MacLaine, one of the playthings. Wilder then made a superb comedy with Lemmon and Walter Matthau, *The Fortune Cookie* (1966), and these two teamed again in Gene Saks' *The Odd Couple* (1968), who share an apartment and some funny contretemps.

Doris Day made some boy-chases-girl comedies with Rock Hudson, *Pillow Talk* (1959) and *Send Me No Flowers* (1964), but the sophisticated Powell/Loy mantle seemed likelier to fall to Jane Fonda and Robert Redford,

with their comedy of the trials of newly-weds, *Barefoot in the. Park* (1967).

British comedy has had some great exponents who usually have not succeeded internationally: Gracie Fields, George Formby, Will Hay were legends in Britain but failed elsewhere. Postwar British comedies meant, first, Ealing Studios, and second, *Carry On*. The Ealing comedies were inventive and well acted. Those starring Alec Guinness, such as *Kind Hearts and Coronets* (1949), *The Lavender Hill Mob* (1951), and *The Man in the White Suit* (1951), were as good as anything being done in Hollywood. The *Carry On* films, immensely popular, are mere ephemeral bawdy exercises in comparison. *Genevieve* (1953), *Tom*

above
The Lavender Hill Mob (1951), whose bank-robbing proceeds are converted into gold replicas of the Eiffel Tower, which fall into innocent hands. Sidney James, Alec Guinness, Alfie Bass and Stanley Holloway in the Ealing comedy.

left
Jacques Tati, whose films as actor-director are gentle criticisms of aspects of modern life. This still is from his second, *Monsieur Hulot's Holiday* (1952).

Jones (1961) and *Billy Liar* (1963)
were successful, and Tony Hancock,
Britain's funniest post-war comedian,
made a very good but underrated film,
The Punch and Judy Man (1963).

A modern clown is Jerry Lewis,
who has his devotees, and *The Nutty
Professor* (1963) has its moments, but
mostly his madness is boring – he is
manic-depressing. Another, quieter,
kettle-of-fish is Jacques Tati, a Frenchman, who like his fellow-countryman,
Fernandel, began on the music halls.
Tati makes few films, but puts years
of work into each, getting his effects

from minute observation of everyday
behaviour, which, slightly exaggerated,
becomes absurd. His hat, pipe, mackin-
tosh and tall figure make a character
as recognizable as Chaplin's clown,
and *Mon Oncle* (1958), his satire on
the plastics and gadgets age, is in the
class of *Modern Times*. Tati is a
spiritual descendant of Linder, and a
true throw-back to the golden age of
silent comedy.

Westerns

They went thataway

The Western is the most typically American of all movie genres. Indeed, it could hardly have originated anywhere else, although it has been taken up since by other nations with a certain measure of success. The typical Western celebrates a specific era in the history of the United States, the 'moving frontier' of nineteenth-century pioneer life anywhere west of St Louis, and it does so via the formula of a set of familiar, though not necessarily immutable, rules and conventions and a series of events which may have had an historic foundation but which have moved a long way from reality.

Many of these conventions made their appearance in the first real Western: Edwin S. Porter's six-minute-long *The Great Train Robbery* (1903). Unlike the numerous vignettes with a Western theme produced by early film-makers hoping to cash in on the success of the enormously popular dime novel, *The Great Train Robbery* had a form. It had a holdup by masked raiders, a fight on the roof of a train, and a gun battle showdown in which the villains received their just deserts, all cleverly edited together by Porter. The film did not have an authentic background, however, having been made in New Jersey.

The first Western star, Broncho Billy Anderson, moved the Western from its early Eastern locations to California and the real West for most of his hundreds of films. Anderson – initials G. M. – became Broncho Billy when a film called *Broncho Billy and the Baby* (1908), which he made himself and in which he took the lead because no-one else was available, became a big success. He was the leading Western star until William S. Hart and Tom Mix and their more sophisticated movies superseded him.

William S. Hart was given his first Western role by Thomas Ince, the producer and director who, with D. W.

left
Nine o'clock hold-up: Edwin S. Porter's
The Great Train Robbery (1903).

above
Dustin Farnum, Princess Red Wing and
Billy Elmer in *The Squaw Man* (1913),
the first of three versions of the story
made by Cecil B. DeMille.

right
One in the eye for a villain from Tom
Mix in *The Broncho Twister*, an early
William Fox film.

TomMix AND TONY THE WONDER HORSE IN WILLIAM FOX PRESENTS HORSEMAN OF THE PLAINS

above
Tom Mix in *Horseman
of the Plains* (1928).

opposite
William S. Hart in *White Oak* (1922).

Griffith, did more than anyone else to give the Western film a shape and style. By the time Hart came on the Western scene in 1914, Griffith had left it and Thomas Ince was nearing the end of his best work. Hart's style, which he created as actor, writer and director, was serious, dedicated and concerned with putting honest reality into the Western. Tom Mix, on the other hand, was much more flamboyant, with a style deriving from the old rodeo shows. His films for Fox, whom he joined in 1917 after a long apprenticeship in minor parts, were full of action, fights and chases, and did not try to raise serious issues. After a time, they made Hart's films seem rather slow and old-fashioned, and when Hart made his last film, the wonderfully epic *Tumbleweeds*, in 1925, the field was left largely to Tom Mix and his 'B' Westerns, and to the Western stars who followed him: Ken Maynard, Hoot Gibson, George O'Brien, Buck Jones, Tim McCoy, William Boyd (Hopalong Cassidy), and later in the 1930s and 40s, singing cowboys like Gene Autrey and Roy Rogers.

Although at this time the Western was considered as little more than escapism by serious movie makers, not all Westerns were 'B' pictures. Apart from Hart's work, many notable films were made after DeMille showed the way to Hollywood with *The Squaw Man* in 1913. *The Spoilers* (1914), based on Rex Beach's novel, had William Farnum playing his first big role. In the mid-1920s came the first Western epics: James Cruze's *The Covered Wagon* (1923) and John Ford's *The Iron Horse* (1924).

The coming of sound was initially a set-back for the big location Western, and schoolboys in the 1930s made do – albeit very happily – with a diet of largely 'B' Westerns, varied with the occasional grand-scale Western such as *Cimarron* (1931), Raoul Walsh's *The Big Trail* (1930) which gave John Wayne his first big role, and, in 1936, DeMille's *The Plainsman* and King Vidor's *The Texas Rangers*.

The Western Passes a Milestone

1939 was a great year for the Western. Two films made then were to be a watershed in the history of the genre. The first was John Ford's *Stagecoach*, considered by many to be the best Western ever made. It re-established the Western as a suitable subject for main feature films, giving it back literacy, a sense of proportion between myth and reality, and real people instead of the cardboard-figure fist-fighters and gunslingers who had peopled so many 'B' Westerns of the 1930s. It also brought John Wayne back from nine years' obscurity to the leading position in American movies he still holds.

The film was John Ford's first sound Western, and he was to follow it with a group of films which earned him recognition as the great romanti-cist and poet of the West. His other Western of 1939 was *Drums Along the Mohawk*, another exceptionally fine film.

George Marshall's *Destry Rides Again*, a spoof Western starring James Stewart and Marlene Dietrich, was the other great Western milestone of 1939. This film brought sex into the Western – 'adult' sex, not the romantic embrace which ended most of Hart's films or the pretty girls who played sisters or daughters to be rescued from

bad situations in many 'B' features.

Where John Ford's film led the way to the Western with a serious theme, such as *The Ox-Bow Incident* (1943), *Broken Arrow* (1950), *High Noon* (1952) and *Shane* (1953), *Destry Rides Again* helped bring sexuality into the Western. There was Jane Russell in *The Outlaw* (1943), for instance, and Jennifer Jones in *Duel in the Sun* (1946).

One should not over-emphasize this new 'adultness' however. Earlier West-erns had looked at important themes seriously. Although *Broken Arrow* and *Run of the Arrow* (1957) were the first films for many years to consider the

58

right
Cecil B. DeMille's *Union Pacific* (1939)
was a flag-waving, action-packed
account of the building of the railroad
across the United States.

plight of the Indian, other directors
before Delmer Daves and Samuel
Fuller had shown an interest in the
subject, notably Thomas Ince in such
films as *The Indian Massacre* (1912)
and *Heart of an Indian* (1913). Lillian
Gish had given a powerful performance in Victor Sjöström's *The Wind*
in 1928, a film which looked at the
psychological stress created by the
harsh environment of the West.

right
One in a long line of Doc Hollidays, Kirk Douglas scents trouble from Lee Van Cleef in *Gunfight at the O.K. Corral* (1957).

below
Tyrone Power as Jesse and Henry Fonda as Frank James in *Jesse James* (1939), directed by Henry King.

opposite
John Wayne, Robert Mitchum and Arthur Hunnicutt in *El Dorado* (1967).

Familiar Names and Places

The ingenuity and variety of treatment which Western films have shown in their use of a few basic themes, employing the same characters and events over and over again, have been the main reasons for the popularity of the genre. Audiences know they are in familiar territory when they watch a Western. Well-known names, scenes and historical events provide a pleasurable sense of anticipation and expectation: one knows what is going to happen when a roughneck or two try to crowd the quiet man at the bar, just as one knows the inevitable outcome of the meeting between the lonely figure walking up Main Street and the man reaching for his gun who suddenly appears ahead of him, or as one knows that the wagon moving West will at some stage be menaced by Indians appearing from nowhere.

These scenes appear so often because they are basic to many of the comparatively few themes used in the Western: the wicked town, be it Dodge City, Tombstone or Deadwood, which the lawman must clean up; the great trek West of wagons, cattle or the railroad; a man's search for the killer of his father or brother, or the kidnapper of a friend's sister or daughter, and the revenge he takes; feuds between families, within the same family, or between groups with opposed ambitions such as sheepmen and cattlemen; a fight between heroes and villains for valuable property, be it a waterhole, a mine or a railroad; wicked whites, speaking with forked tongues, and stirring up the Indians. Such basic themes have been used to accommodate any number of story lines.

right
Paul Newman played William Bonney –
Billy the Kid – in Arthur Penn's *The
Left-Handed Gun* (1958).

below
The first cattle drive on the Chisholm
Trail was the context of Howard
Hawks' *Red River* (1948).

opposite
The end of the confrontation in the
dusty main street of *High Noon* (1952):
Grace Kelly and Gary Cooper, who won
an Academy Award for his performance
as the sheriff, Kane.

Many of the characters who play out these themes are familiar, too. Given that one actor or one director will interpret a part differently from another, it is also true that as Westerns have come to be used by directors and writers as a vehicle for their thoughts and ideas about the American way of life as a whole, or as a mirror for current American politics, both national and international, so their treatment of characters and events has altered.

The ageing blond General Custer, making his last stand with a megalomaniac gleam in his eye in *Little Big Man* (1970) is a far cry from the dashing soldier played by Errol Flynn in *They Died With Their Boots On* (1941). Handsome, if wooden, Cesar Romero in *Frontier Marshall* (1939) is a different Doc Holliday from Victor Mature's tubercular character in Ford's *My Darling Clementine* (1946), or Kirk Douglas in *Gunfight at the OK Corral* (1957), or the unattractive, rather sordid figure in Frank Perry's *Doc* (1971).

The characters of the Wyatt Earp/Doc Holliday story have been used in other films, from the Gordon Elliott vehicle, *In Old Arizona* (1929), and Edward Cahn's *Law and Order* (1932) to *Wichita* (1955) and *Hour of the Gun* (1967), and by John Ford again in a scene in *Cheyenne Autumn* (1964).

Two other characters whose story (in which Doc Holliday also turns up) has been repeated many times are Sheriff Pat Garrett and William Bonney – 'Billy the Kid'. King Vidor used the real location of the Lincoln County wars for his version of *Billy the Kid* in 1930. Robert Taylor was a rather too smooth *Billy the Kid* in 1941, and Jack Buetel made him an unpleasant character in *The Outlaw* (1943). ('Billy! Let me go!' cried the voluptuous Jane Russell on a poster for this notorious film.) Audie Murphy played Billy in *The Kid from Texas* (1950) and Paul Newman in *The Left-Handed Gun* (1958). There was even a *Billy the Kid versus Dracula* in 1965. John Wayne was the Kid's friend in *Chisum* (1970), and Sam Peckinpah made *Pat Garrett and Billy the Kid* in 1973.

The James brothers have been the subject of several films, including *Jesse James* (1939). Other characters forming part of the familiar world of the Western include Bat Masterson, Wild Bill Hickok, Judge Roy Bean (and Lily Langtry), Buffalo Bill, Kit Carson and Daniel Boon.

The Western Now

The Western has undergone many changes since the Second World War. No longer a simple uncomplicated story of good versus bad, the Western has become psychological, political, allegorical, comic, or, most recently, nostalgic.

In the early 1940s the Western could claim only one major star, John Wayne, and one prominent director, John Ford. Ford made *My Darling Clementine* in 1946, and followed it with his finest Westerns: *Fort Apache* and *Three Godfathers* (1948), *She Wore a Yellow Ribbon* (1949), *Wagonmaster* and *Rio Grande* (1950) and *The Searchers* (1956). John Wayne was in all but two of them.

In 1948, Howard Hawks made his first big Western after a long career as a distinguished director. His *Red River* was a major contribution to the Western genre. It, and his later *Rio Bravo* (1959) and *El Dorado* (1967), have helped turn him into a 'cult' Western director rivalling the towering figure of John Ford. Whereas Ford's films are marked by a poetic romanticism, Hawks's are distinguished by the stern professionalism, untouched by sentiment, of his characters.

Two other major Western directors of the 1950s, Anthony Mann and Budd Boetticher, each made several films which have since grown in critical estimation. Mann starred James Stewart in most of his films, and Budd Boetticher used Randolph Scott in his.

far left
Jennifer Jones in *Duel in the Sun*
(1946).

left
The Magnificent Seven: from left to
right, Yul Brynner, Steve McQueen,
Horst Buchholz, Charles Bronson,
Robert Vaughn, Brad Dexter and James
Coburn.

below
James Stewart and Debra Paget in
Broken Arrow (1950).

above
Van Heflin and Alan Ladd in *Shane* (1953).

left
John Ford's *The Searchers* (1956) gave John Wayne, seen here with Jeffrey Hunter, the opportunity to give a superb performance as Ethan Edwards, the loner.

Two films of the 1950s which were to have a strong influence on the direction taken by the Western were both made by directors new to the genre, and who have not since made another Western. Fred Zinnemann's *High Noon* (1952) has been seen as an allegory of the McCarthy era in the United States, and had Gary Cooper as the man standing alone and outnumbered against the villains. *Shane* (1953), George Stevens's one Western, also featured a loner – Alan Ladd –

sorting out the problems of a group of people and then riding away. Films like these, or Henry King's *The Gunfighter* (1950), ensured that the Western, whatever direction it took, could no longer be considered just a form of low- or middle-brow entertainment.

The late 1950s and early 1960s were characterized for the Western by several successful epics, including *The Big Country* (1958), *The Alamo* (1960), which was John Wayne's first venture into directing, and *The Magnificent Seven* (1960), and by a move to Westerns with contemporary settings: *The Misfits* (1961), the last completed film for two of its stars, Marilyn Monroe and Clark Gable, *Lonely Are The Brave* (1962) with Kirk Douglas, and *Hud* (1963) which starred Paul Newman and Melvyn Douglas.

The rapid success of the television Western has not only usurped the role

above
The bloody end of Warren Oates and Ben Johnson in Peckinpah's *The Wild Bunch* (1969), a film which began a series of similar, but largely inferior, violent Westerns.

top
Robert Redford and Paul Newman in *Butch Cassidy and the Sundance Kid* (1969).

opposite
Dustin Hoffman about to use his Bowie knife in *Little Big Man* (1970).

of the 'B' feature Western, which was still being competently handled by stars like Randolph Scott and Joel McCrea in the 1950s, but has also given the main feature Western problems. There are fewer Westerns being made now than before, and quite a number of them are characterized by a nostalgia for the passing of the West.

Sam Peckinpah's *Ride the High Country* (1962 *Guns in the Afternoon* in the U.K.) was about two old-timers for whom time had just about run out, and was a superb film, giving great roles to Randolph Scott and Joel McCrea. Peckinpah's *The Wild Bunch* (1969) was also about men for whom the sands have run out. This time their end was violent and exceptionally bloody. The end of *Butch Cassidy and the Sundance Kid* (1969) was also violent and bloody, but romanticized by the insouciant charm of Paul Newman and Robert Redford.

Romance

Here's looking at you, kid!

'It took more than one man to change my name to Shanghai Lily.' Marlene Dietrich playing that grand old stand-by, the Lady with a Past, in *Shanghai Express* (1932). Warner Oland was the devilish Communist.

There is a moment at the end of *Queen Christina* when Garbo, queen no longer, steps up into the prow of the ship bound for Spain. This is the last we see of her, and she stands expressionless, gazing out over the water, behind her a kingdom and a lover lost, in front who knows? It is one of the cinema's supreme romantic images and it works because into that sweet vacancy we pour all our own griefs and hopes of renewal. Why? Well, the theme's a cinch of course – all for love has been slaying them for generations. But it's the star too. Garbo seems to have realized instinctively that understatement extended rather than limited a performance. The enigmatic quality in all her mature work invites audience identification and it's right there that the subtle alchemy of wish-fulfilment begins. The romantic movie is not interested in life as it is but in life as its audiences dream it might be.

That doesn't mean it has to be roses all the way. Most of the great romantic themes are tragic, but it's tragedy rounded out, made smooth. People suffer but they do it beautifully. They exult; they don't moan and bitch and refuse to pass the marmalade. 'Here's looking at you, kid,' says Bogart to Ingrid Bergman at the end of *Casablanca* (1942). Duty and husband have won out; love and happiness are renounced in a laconic farewell. Love denied is also the theme of *Camille* (1936), with dying courtesan Garbo rejecting young lover Robert Taylor lest she ruin his promising career; of *The Dark Angel* (1925), in which Ronald Colman, blinded in the First World War, conceals his plight and lets Vilma Banky find happiness with their best friend; and of *Possessed* (1931), where Clark Gable turns the tables when he comes after mistress Joan Crawford having found out she's left him because she believes their affair may wreck his hopes of becoming governor.

The noble sacrifice of mother love has been another constant theme in

above
Naughty lady, British style. Murder, highway robbery, and James Mason give Margaret Lockwood her kicks in *The Wicked Lady* (1945).

right
Jennifer Jones and lover Charlton Heston in *Ruby Gentry* (1952), the story of a woman with just one aim — 'to wreck a whole town sin by sin, man by man'.

the romantic cinema. *Madame X*, *Stella Dallas*, and *Imitation of Life* are archetypal, each having been made several times (*Madame X* holds the record with five re-makes), but the also-rans include *Humoresque* (1920), *The Sin of Madelon Claudet* (1931), *Millie* (1931), *The Strange Case of Clara Deane* (1932), *Call Her Savage* (1932), *Wicked Woman* (1935), and *Primrose Path* (1940). Mother would murder to protect her children from scandal or from a brutal husband, and even (oh, fate worse than death!) she walked the streets to keep them from starvation. Sometimes she was separated from them in early childhood due to some misdemeanour and found them again at the last; 'Let me hold you for a moment as if you were my son,' says Madame X and dies unrecognized.

Of course there are lovers too who think the world well lost for love: *Queen Christina* (1933), renouncing her kingdom; nightclub singer Marlene Dietrich, barefoot and evening-gowned, stalking off into the deserts of *Morocco* (1930); *Anna Karenina* (Garbo in 1927 and 1935, Vivien Leigh in 1948), played against Tolstoy's text in a full-blown celebration of romantic

above
Dolores Costello has to make do with John 'The Great Profile' Barrymore's other side in *When a Man Loves* (1927).

right
Valentino, the screen's greatest lover in his most famous role.

72

73

love; Charles Boyer as Crown Prince Rudolph and Danielle Darrieux as mistress Maria Vetsera, choosing suicide in the hunting lodge at *Mayerling* (1936); Irene Dunne (1932), Margaret Sullavan (1941), and Susan Hayward (1961), all forsaking hopes of marriage and children to live as the *Back Street* mistress of a married man. Sullavan suffered rather well and she'd already sacrificed all for a brief whirl with John Boles in *Only Yesterday* (1933) and then, as the tubercular wife in *Three Comrades* (1938), she'd laid down her life so that husband Robert Taylor could make a fresh start. Others trade position for just a brief respite from life and then return regretfully to the old ways. Elinor Glyn's legendary *Three Weeks* (1924) are spent on tiger skins and beds of immaculate roses, she (Aileen Pringle) queen of some Ruritanian kingdom and he (Conrad Nagel) a young Britisher of noble birth. Almost thirty years later princess Audrey Hepburn's on the same kick when she meets up with American journalist Gregory Peck on an incognito *Roman Holiday* (1953). Society being what it is, men seem to have their cake and eat it rather more effectively. *Viz* Nelson's grand passion: just the thing for a succession of 'great hero and *grande amoureuse*' dramas which began in 1921 with *Lady Hamilton* and continued right down to the cynical old 1970s with *The Divine Lady* (1928), *That Hamilton Woman* (1941), *Emma Hamilton* (1969), and *A Bequest to the Nation* (1973).

top right
Camille (Greta Garbo) and her young lover Armand, played by Robert Taylor (1936).

right
Just a *Brief Encounter* for Celia Johnson and Trevor Howard (1945).

IPL 26-24.

But parting being such sweet sorrow, it tends to get higher coverage. Exquisite was the agony amongst the teacups and the sticky buns as Celia Johnson and Trevor Howard gave passion the go-by in *Brief Encounter* (1945). And Garbo spent a sizeable part of her early career being rejected by men who'd found out about her lurid past; in *Susan Lenox: Her Fall and Rise* (1931) she goes to the bad in a really big way but still she keeps on loving Clark Gable. With Lillian Gish unfulfilled love sometimes had more Freudian undertones. As *The White Sister* (1923) she takes the veil thinking her sweetheart has died in battle, and it's a flood that snatches her away from some awkward decision-making when he turns up again. Death intervenes in Visconti's elegiac *Death in Venice*

(1971) too, but the beautiful boy who haunts the dying composer represents not just love but the whole area of ecstatic experience which as artist and man he has denied.

The fatal relationship is another hardy annual. There's Theda Bara crying, 'Kiss me, fool', as she completes her lover's degradation in *A Fool There Was* (1914); the mysterious Garance (Arletty) of *Les Enfants du Paradis* (1944), for whom Baptiste (Jean-Louis Barrault) abandons wife and career; Charles Boyer as big-time gangster Pépé le Moko in *Algiers* (1938), falling for society-girl Hedy Lamarr and getting shot up when he tries to follow her to France; and Gene Tierney playing poor mad Ellen Berent in *Leave Her to Heaven* (1945), so obsessed with her husband that

far right
The 1957 remake of Hemingway's *A Farewell to Arms*. This version starred Rock Hudson as the American who joined the International Brigade during the Spanish Civil War and Jennifer Jones as the woman he loves.

right
The 1973 remake of *The Great Gatsby*, with Robert Redford and Mia Farrow: 'his dream must have seemed so close that he could hardly fail to grasp it'.

opposite
A production still from *Flesh and the Devil* (1927). Garbo and Gilbert were the great romantic team of the 1920s. Helped not a little by rumours of an off-screen affair, their three silents together did well at the box-office.

left
Ronald Colman and Vilma Banky in *The Night of Love* (1927). The other big partnership of the 1920s, their basically tender relationship contrasted with the tormented passion of the Garbo-Gilbert combo.

below
Spencer Tracy and Katharine Hepburn in *Keeper of the Flame* (1942). This was drama, but most of their films were comedy and it was a new kind of romance — the sparring of equals.

she kills her brother-in-law, aborts her own child, and makes her suicide look like the work of her half-sister.

The terrible face of love indeed! But there's an equally healthy sub-genre intent on convincing us that love is the great redeemer. In the shape of Robert Browning it rescues a minor Victorian poetess from life as a semi-invalid in *The Barretts of Wimpole Street* (1937 and 1957), and when a cynical playboy goes religious after accidentally blinding a young widow, what more likely than that he should turn surgeon and restore her sight? *Magnificent Obsession* (1935 and 1954) was the name, and the incumbents Robert Taylor and Rock Hudson. In *Unfinished Business* (1941) Irene Dunne's husband kicks alcoholism under her influence, and some inspired casting in *The African Queen* (1951) has prissy missionary Katharine Hepburn and drunken boatman Humphrey Bogart succumbing to the old black magic. Amnesia is the problem in *Random Harvest* (1942), but Greer Garson's devoted nursing brings husband Ronald Colman back to health again and she marries him a second time—without him realizing it!

Sometimes love's power transcends even death. Kay Francis and William Powell meet and fall in love on a *One Way Passage* to New York (1932); they agree to meet again in six months' time though it can never be for she is dying and he sentenced to death. The six months pass, and come midnight on the appointed day in the bar where they would have met two champagne glasses shatter and the stems are

found crossed . . . it's their sign of course. Love beyond the grave is also the theme of *Portrait of Jenny* (1948), which has artist Joseph Cotten falling in love with Jennifer Jones, his ghostly young sitter, and of *Pandora and the Flying Dutchman* (1950), where Ava Gardner sails away with James Mason, the man condemned to search down the centuries for a woman prepared to die for him.

Most of the movies described here were deplored by the critics. They were 'the women's weepies'. One sub-genre that had built-in man appeal was the romantic adventure film. The swashbucklers of the costume dramas might love – though honour or devilment were equally likely to be their motive – but it was the swordplay and the acrobatics that were their *raison d'être*. Douglas Fairbanks confounding eight men with his dazzling swordsmanship in *The Black Pirate* (1926), Ronald Colman as Rudolph Rassendyll coming face to face with the villainous Rupert of Hentzau in *The Prisoner of Zenda* (1937), Errol Flynn playing *Captain Blood* (1935), the physician cum slave cum pirate who ends up governor of Jamaica, Tyrone Power preserving the family honour in *The Mark of Zorro* (1940), and Burt Lancaster, the last of the breed, swinging through the rigging in *The Crimson Pirate* (1952): it was bravura athletics which brought the audiences in, and kept them there – to dream.

below
Errol Flynn as *The Sea Hawk* (1940), in a story loosely, very loosely, based on Rafael Sabatini's yarn about a family in the days of the first Elizabeth.

right
Third time around for *The Prisoner of Zenda* (1952). Stewart Granger played the dual role of Rudolph Rassendyll/King Rudolf, and Deborah Kerr the princess.

874

War

What price glory?

The cinema and modern warfare were born at much the same time, two products of the nineteenth-century technological revolution. It is not surprising that more movies should have been made about war than about any other subject – spectacular and violent, adventurous and exciting, horrifying in its finality, war is also an ideal base for serious comment on the progress – or lack of it – of civilization, of man's inhumanity to man, or of the reactions of men and women plunged into the maelstrom of conflict.

On a practical level, war has been an important factor in the progress and development of the cinema, both technically and in its use of subject matter. The Great War demonstrated the huge potential of film as a propaganda weapon and as a medium of mass education, while it also gave the cinema the social and intellectual respectability it had previously lacked. Technically, the demands of war photography helped refine and extend the uses of the camera and were also – notably in the U.S. Army Signal Corps

– a training ground for the film-making talents which would emerge once the war was over.

The general standard of feature films about war made during the First World War, with the exception of a few films like the Chaplin masterpiece *Shoulder Arms* (1918), Herbert Brenon's *War Brides* (1916) or Thomas Ince's *Civilization* (1916), was not very high. The cinema had to wait until men who had fought in and understood the horrors of trench warfare returned to film-making before its

opposite
The ghosts of the dead walk in Abel
Gance's *J'Accuse* (1919).

left
Tom O'Brien and John Gilbert in *The
Big Parade* (1925).

below
Rudolph Valentino in *The Four
Horsemen of the Apocalypse* (1921).

finest comments on the War to end Wars were made.

The Frenchman Abel Gance was one such man. Nine of his ten closest friends died in the war, and the futile waste of their lives was one of the reasons for his making *J'Accuse* (1919), the first great pacifist film of the Great War. Most of it was filmed during the war and Gance used men on leave from the Front in some of its scenes.

Rex Ingram's *The Four Horsemen of the Apocalypse* (1921) appeared when films about the war were box-office poison, and much of its huge success was due to the magnetic presence of Rudolph Valentino in his first major film, but the film also had splendidly realistic battle scenes and strong patriotic overtones.

By the mid-1920s, war was once again a major subject for film. Among

many fine American films of this time, King Vidor's *The Big Parade* (1925) stood out as a sincerely objective account of what fighting in the Great War really meant. Raoul Walsh's *What Price Glory?* was another box-office hit of the time, whereas D. W. Griffith's last major film, *Isn't Life Wonderful?*, was not, largely because it asked for sympathy for the defeated Germany. The war in the air provided the motif

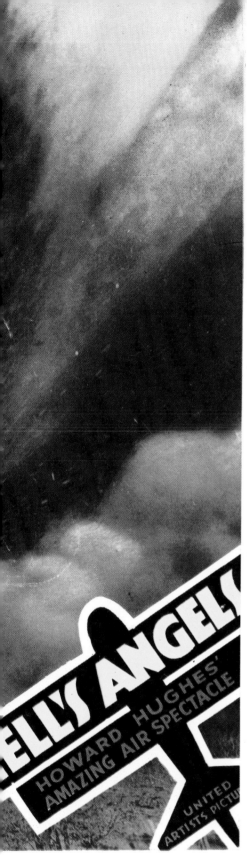

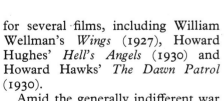

left
Howard Hughes' *Hell's Angels* (1930).

below
John Guillermin's *The Blue Max* (1966)
is one of the few recent films to have
been about the First World War.

bottom
Gary Cooper and Richard Arlen in
Wings (1927).

for several films, including William
Wellman's *Wings* (1927), Howard
Hughes' *Hell's Angels* (1930) and
Howard Hawks' *The Dawn Patrol*
(1930).

Amid the generally indifferent war
films being made in Britain at this
time, Maurice Elvey's work stood out
for its sincerity and technical skill,
qualities well demonstrated in his
Mademoiselle from Armentières (1926).

War as News and Documentary

above
Target for Tonight (1941) was a fine account by Harry Watt of an R.A.F. bombing raid over Germany.

opposite top
Jean Grémillon's *Six Juin à l'Aube* (1945) described the Normandy Landings and their aftermath.

opposite bottom
The Battle of Russia (1942) one of the war-time 'Why We Fight' series made by Frank Capra to promote public knowledge and understanding of the reasons for fighting.

The Boer War in South Africa, which began in 1899, was a major subject of the first newsreels, and reportage and documentary have been an historically important part of war film output ever since. In the hands of men like Joseph Rosenthal, the early camera recorded for posterity – and for the entertainment of cinema audiences at home – events of the Boer War, the Boxer Rebellion, the Russo-Japanese War and the Spanish-American War, as well as conflicts and skirmishes from Belfast to the Balkans.

The newsreel was very popular during the 1914–18 War, especially in Britain, and much of the film, acquired often at the expense of the lives of the cameramen, was used in compilation films of major events. Geoffrey Malins and J. B. McDowell were two British film-makers whose First World War compilations were successful and influential, notably in such films as *The Battle of the Somme* (1916) and *The Battle of Arras*.

While the First World War was a great stimulus to the development of the newsreel, the Second World War mobilized the documentary for some of its finest work. Much of the superb, historically important film shot during the war by American, British, Russian, German and other combatants has since formed the basis of major television documentaries. But much else was used at the time to create some of the best and most enduring films of the war, which set out to record it, or to inform, persuade and boost the morale of citizens at home and the troops in the battle zones.

Frank Capra's *Why We Fight* series, Carol Reed's and Garson Kanin's *The True Glory* (1945), the many outstanding British war-time documentaries from the Cavalcanti and Jennings film, *The First Days* (1940), and *Squadron 922* (1940) to *Western Approaches* (1944), Dovzhenko's and Solntseva's *The Battle for the Ukraine* (1943), and Jean Grémillon's *Le Six Juin à l'Aube* (1945), are just a sample of the superb film documentation of the Second World War.

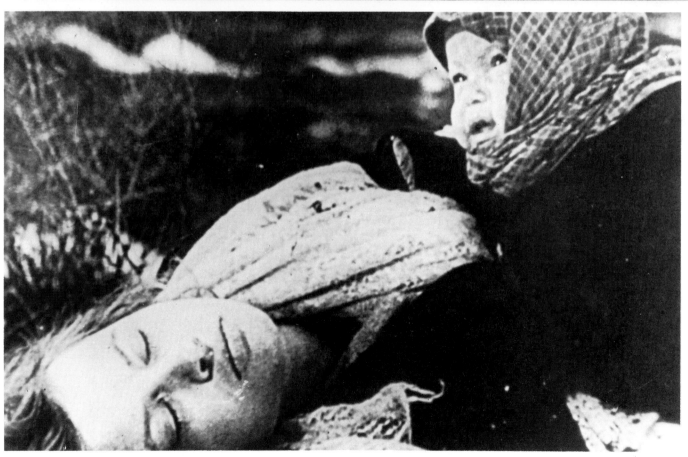

The Cinema Against War

It is often said that the greatest war films have all been anti-war films. Perhaps it is true to say that a film which sets out honestly to convey the reality of war, and the effect that it has on people caught up in its horrors, will be a statement against war. This is as true of *M*A*S*H* (1969) a riotous, blood-splattered comedy in which no-one 'goes over the top' or does anything particularly heroic, as it is of *All Quiet on the Western Front* (1930).

Abel Gance's *J'Accuse* apart, Lewis Milestone's *All Quiet on the Western Front* was one of the first major pacifist statements of the cinema. It considered the brutality of war through the gradual demoralization and eventual death of a unit of young German troops, and was more poetic in its treatment than was the German G. W. Pabst's stark, sombre and brilliant account of four soldiers on the French front, *Westfront 1918*, also made in 1930 and also, like *All Quiet . . .*, given a hostile reception in Germany. Another fine anti-war film of this year was *Tell England*, the work of the English director, Anthony Asquith.

Jean Renoir's *La Grande Illusion* (1936) was a last great cry against war before the anti-war theme was swept aside in the tide of jingoism, patriotism and nationalism which dominated war films when the renewal of conflict became more and more inevitable as the 1930s ended. Renoir's film – unusually for a film about the First World War – was set in a prisoner-of-war camp where the boundaries of class and nationality were shown to mean little or nothing in terms of human relationships.

There have been many fine anti-war films since the end of the Second World War, including two which took as their theme soldiers of the First World War shot for desertion or cowardice: Stanley Kubrick's *Paths of Glory* (1957) and Joseph Losey's *King and Country* (1964); and several which have looked at the horrors of nuclear war, including Kubrick's *Dr Strangelove, or How I Learned to Stop Worrying and Love the Bomb* (1963), and Peter Watkins' *The War Game* (1965), made for television but so horrifying that the BBC would not show it.

But it is doubtful that any film, however realistic or horrifying, could prevent a war. When Gance's *J'Accuse* was shown in 1919, some-one said that if it had appeared in 1913 it might have prevented the war. Jean Renoir showed less illusions about the power of the cinema when he told the writer, Robert Hughes, in an often-quoted remark, 'In 1936 I made a picture named *La Grande Illusion* in which I tried to express all my deep feelings for the cause of peace. This film was very successful. Three years later the war broke out.'

right
Director Carl Foreman planned *The Victors* (1963) as the ultimate anti-war film. Its stars were George Hamilton (*left*) and George Peppard (*centre*).

below
Lewis Milestone's *All Quiet on the Western Front* (1930).

The Second World War and After

As in the First World War, the style, content and quality of feature films were greatly influenced by conditions and events during the Second World War.

This was most marked at first in Britain, where a revitalized film industry, much influenced by its documentary tradition, produced a series of feature films about the war and its effect on the men and women fighting it on the Home Front and in the Forces, which remains a truthful, realistic record of a nation at war. At first, these films were often about the adventure and heroism of war; but as the war dragged on, film-makers turned their attention more to the effect war had on individuals, in such films as Launder and Gilliat's *Millions Like Us* (1943) and Asquith's *The Way to the Stars* (1945). The restrained realism which characterized most of these films was still in evidence in one or two of the films of the 1950s war film revival in Britain – Charles Frend's film of the Nicholas Monsarrat novel, *The Cruel Sea* (1953) being outstanding among them – but many of the films of this period were about stiff-upper-lip heroics in P.O.W. camps and the like, and lacked the quality of the best of the war-time films.

In occupied France, film-makers kept away from contemporary subjects and turned instead to a romantic style from which men like Marcel Carné (*Les Enfants du Paradis*), Cocteau and Bresson created some of the most exciting fantasies in film history. For the German film industry, the war meant a vast output of propaganda films, aimed at the home market and at the occupied countries, including the technically brilliant but vicious in sentiment *The Eternal Jew* and *Jud Süss*.

The American film industry was not much affected by the war at first, and its studio and star systems carried on as before, even though many of Hollywood's leading stars joined up to do their bit. Stars like John Wayne and Errol Flynn were seen doing their bit, winning the war single-handed, or so it seemed, in many of the adventure films which were a staple of American war-film production in the early years of the war. Among films made to increase support for America's allies, William Wyler's *Mrs Miniver* (1942) enjoyed an enormous success. Towards the end of the war, American directors began taking a more sober and realistic look at the effect the war was having on their country's people

left
Burgess Meredith as Ernie Pyle (*right*) pauses by the body of Captain Walker (Robert Mitchum) in *The Story of G.I. Joe* (1945).

right
Errol Flynn sets out to re-take Burma in Raoul Walsh's *Objective, Burma!* (1945). Henry Hull (*rear*) looks on.

below
Roberto Rossellini's *Paisà* (1946) was concerned with the effects of war on ordinary people. Maria Michi played a girl forced by the circumstances of war into prostitution.

Anthony Quinn in David Lean's *Lawrence of Arabia* (1962).

and would continue to have long after the war was over. Among many fine films made at this time, Ford's *They Were Expendable*, Milestone's *A Walk in the Sun*, William Wellman's *The Story of G.I. Joe* (all made in 1945) and Wyler's *The Best Years of Our Lives* (1946), were all outstanding.

The cinema's response to war has been fed constantly by the real thing since 1945 – Korea, Vietnam, the Middle East have all been the settings for war films – and by the threat of nuclear holocaust. Among the hundreds of war films made simply for mass entertainment – and the makers' profit, for war remains one of the most popular movie themes – have been many of epic proportions, like the hugely popular *The Bridge on the River*

Kwai (1957), *The Longest Day* (1962), *The Victors* (1963), and *Patton: Lust for Glory* (1969) in which George C. Scott gave a well-observed study of the U.S. general. Many others, like Robert Aldrich's *The Dirty Dozen* (1967) have exploited the violence of war, while others have been the work of people using film to make pacifist, anti-militarist statements which the world will see, even if it does not heed their message.

above
George C. Scott as the famous U.S. General in *Patton: Lust for Glory* (1969).

right
A Last Supper for the Painless Pole (John Schuck) in Robert Altman's *M*A*S*H* (1969). Sharing the feast are Carl Gottlieb, David Arkin, Tom Skerritt, Donald Sutherland and Elliot Gould.

Documentary Films

The creative treatment of actuality

'Documentary' was a term coined in the 1920s by the Scottish pioneer documentary-maker, John Grierson. He defined documentary as 'the creative treatment of actuality' – the reporting camera plus the individual interpretation of the film-maker. It was such creative treatment that made Robert J. Flaherty's masterpieces *Nanook of the North* (1922) and *Moana* (1925) the earliest documentaries, and not just superior travelogues.

In Britain in the 1930s, documentary-making became a distinct movement. It was the country's first individual film tradition, and its major contribution to the art of the film. Good factual films had been made in Britain in the early days of the

Robert J. Flaherty's *Nanook of the North* (1922).

silent film, notably Herbert Ponting's record of Scott's Antarctic expedition between 1910 and 1913, and Geoffrey Malins' and J. B. McDowell's *The Battle of the Somme* (1916). But the work of such men as Grierson, Basil Wright, Paul Rotha, Alberto Cavalcanti, Harry Watt and the poetically brilliant Humphrey Jennings was characterized by a social purpose which showed the reality of life in Britain in a way that most feature films of the time did not. Most of these documentaries were sponsored by government bodies such as the Gen-

eral Post Office or the Empire Marketing Board, and later by private companies.

The Soviet Union is the only other country to have developed a unified documentary movement. In the 1920s a large number of important documentaries were made, most of them having a propaganda purpose. Among them Eisenstein's *Battleship Potemkin* (1925) must be included, although it was a reconstruction of events rather than a first-hand account of them. Esther Shub used archive film to make *The Fall of the Romanov Dynasty* (1927) and *The Russia of Nikolai II and Lev Tolstoy* (1928). Other documentaries, all made in 1929, were Eisenstein's *The General Line*, about

top
John Grierson's *Drifters* (1929), the first major film of the British documentary movement, was about the Scottish herring fleet.

above
Housing Problems (1935) was filmed by Arthur Elton and Edgar Anstey in the slums of Stepney, London.

above
Olympische Spiele, Leni Riefenstahl's brilliant four-hour film of the 1936 Berlin Olympic Games, took two years to edit from the hundreds of thousands of feet of film shot by over thirty cameramen and automatic cameras.

right
Mike Wadleigh's film of a three-day pop festival *Woodstock* (1970) became a celebration of rock culture.

the collectivization of farms, Dziga Vertov's *Man with a Movie Camera* and Viktor Turin's beautifully photographed film of the building of the trans-Siberian railway, *Turksib*.

Other national film industries with outstanding documentaries to their credit include Germany, where Leni Riefenstahl's *Triumph of the Will* (1934) and *Olympische Spiele 1936* (1938) stood out in an otherwise drear period; and Canada, where John Grierson went in 1940 to head the new National Film Board. The tradition established then was still apparent in the remarkable 1966 documentary, *Warrendale*, filmed in a Toronto home for mentally handicapped children.

The Brazilian director, Alberto Cavalcanti, was an important influence on the early British documentary movement, both via his film *Rien que les Heures* (1926) which showed life in Paris over 24 hours, and for the work he did in England for the GPO film unit and for Ealing. Another French-language documentary of awesome power was Alain Resnais' film about the German concentration camps, *Nuit et Brouillard* (1955).

In the United States, apart from the work of Robert Flaherty, whose last film was the poetic *Louisiana Story* (1948), the documentary tradition was not strong until the Second World War. In the 1930s many films, including

Pare Lorentz' work *The Plow that Broke the Plain* (1936) and *The River* (1937) were government-sponsored. The *March of Time* series, which was widely shown outside the United States, was sponsored by Time magazine. The *Why We Fight* series, to which many well-known feature directors contributed, was one of the outstanding documentary series of the Second World War. Totally different and a big box office success was *Woodstock* (1970), while in the U.S. today Robert Flaherty's tradition lives on in the work of Frederick Wiseman, who has been making a remarkable series of films about American institutions.

Crime

Little Caesar starts a crime wave

Organized crime in America boomed with the unenforceable Volstead Law of 1920 which prohibited the sale and consumption of intoxicating drink. The activities of bootleggers and their mobs became notorious and provided excellent raw material for the film. Hollywood faced its own prohibition in 1930: the Hays Code decreed that film gangsters, unlike real gangsters, were not allowed to profit from their crimes. These two sanctions shaped the early crime films.

The first gangster film to make a big impact on the public was Josef von Sternberg's *Underworld* (1927). Written by Ben Hecht, and produced in four weeks without big stars, it played to capacity audiences and revealed a public curiosity in the lives of gangsters. Al Capone's slaughter of a rival gang in the St Valentine's Day Massacre of 1929, and the stock market

above
Clive Brook and Evelyn Brent in the first successful gangster film, Josef von Sternberg's *Underworld* (1927).

right
The guns, the hats, the ornate scenery and the immaculate dress of the archetypal gangster leader, Edward G. Robinson in *Little Caesar* (1930).

crash which enabled the mobs to move in on big business, kept the underworld in the headlines and led to a conventional style of movie.

The film which set the pattern was the early talkie, *Little Caesar* (1930), directed by Mervyn Le Roy. It established one of the great gangster actors, Edward G. Robinson, whose Rico Bandello shared characteristics with Capone. The story became typical: hoodlum dreams of the big-time with its trappings, power, wealth and glam-

Jason Robards appears to be somewhat
upset by some wilful destruction in *The
St Valentine's Day Massacre* (1967).

left
James Cagney's treatment of Mae Clarke in *The Public Enemy* (1931), when he pushed grapefruit into her face, established him as a tough-guy figure.

right
A shootout in *Scarface* (1932), with the gangsters using cars as cover. In front are Paul Muni and Vince Bennett.

our; by ruthlessness, double-cross and the 'shoot first, argue later' technique, he works his way up, only to meet a spectacular end in the last reel (the Hays Code in operation). In Rico's case, he was shot through an advertisement hoarding, asking plaintively 'Is this the end of Rico?'. It was only the beginning. *The Public Enemy* (1931), directed by William Wellman, saw James Cagney repeat the formula. From youthful petty thieving, he graduates to shooting his mentor, gets his tuxedo and his girl, sees his friend mown down by a rival gang, and ends as a corpse falling through his mother's door. The following year, Howard Hawks' *Scarface* (1932) starred Paul Muni as Tony Camonte (again with suggestions of Capone, who had a scar). He meets his end in a last scene shootout with limousines as cover, adding another cliché to the genre. Censorship problems affected *Scar-*

face; scenes had to be cut to make the criminal less sympathetic. The emphasis in gangster films shifted to the cop and Cagney and Robinson temporarily changed sides. Cagney played one of J. Edgar Hoover's *G-Men* (1935), which used another convention: the liberal use of newspaper headlines to speed the action. Edward G. in *Bullets or Ballots* (1936) played a cop who joins the crooks in order to expose them. In this film 'respectable' bankers are among the racketeers operating a multi-million dollar extortion business. Whether by accident or design the film exposed the extent to which organized crime had permeated American life.

A message of a different sort was contained in Fritz Lang's *M* (1931), a German film in which Peter Lorre was a child murderer based on the notorious Kürten. The underworld resolve to catch him, and the ensuing

chase, capture and trial in an old distillery are brilliantly filmed. The death sentence is not carried out, however, as the police arrive to ensure that the psychotic murderer has a legal trial. The moral, in a postscript, that we should guard our children, spoils the final scene.

By the end of the 1930s, Hollywood could look back with nostalgia at the bootlegging era, and Raoul Walsh's *The Roaring Twenties* (1939) depicted a sympathetic bootlegger, James Cagney, contrasted with the more conventional crook, his partner Humphrey Bogart. Cagney is driven to crime by unemployment, and is not a natural hoodlum, but the Hays Code prescribed his fate. In another dramatic end he dies on some church steps, with his girl speaking his epitaph to a cop: 'He used to be a big shot'. In *Angels with Dirty Faces* (1938), Cagney obeys the pleas of his schoolboy friend,

a priest played by Pat O'Brien, to pretend to crack up as he is led to the electric chair, so that the boys who idolize him would learn of the shame of their gangster hero. Cagney's most spectacular end, however, occurred in *White Heat* (1949). As a gangster trapped on top of some huge storage tanks containing inflammatory liquid, he goes up in a great conflagration, crying to his dead Ma that at last he's on top of the world.

A comedy, *Brother Orchid* (1940), starring Edward G. Robinson and Humphrey Bogart, began like a conventional crime movie, but when Edward G., the chief gangster, avoids being bumped off after being 'taken for a ride', to find himself cared for by monks who convert him to God's service, the resulting fun exposed the clichés of the mob film, which could never be quite the same again.

However, the private eye movie arrived with John Huston's *The Maltese Falcon* (1942), in which Humphrey Bogart gave one of his finest performances as Sam Spade, the private eye from Dashiell Hammett's novel. His rasping sibilant voice, curious heartless chuckle, air of menace and demeanour of a man who has seen it all but would not waste words on it, were exactly right for the private eye whose morals are slightly blurred at the edges. Bogart reaffirmed his excellence as another private eye, Raymond Chandler's Philip Marlowe in *The Big Sleep* (1946). The impact of the film came from its rich array of criminal characters, some outlandish scenes and superb racy dialogue, particularly from Bogart and Lauren Bacall.

A psychological twist was introduced in *Laura* (1944), in which Dana Andrews as a detective investigating the 'death' of Gene Tierney, falls in love with her portrait. Miss Tierney arrives at her flat to surprise him reading her correspondence. Andrews' private feelings complicated his role

left
Humphrey Bogart as a gangster leader with his lieutenant George E. Stone in *Bullets or Ballots* (1936).

top right
James Cagney with his gang of worshipping juveniles in *Angels with Dirty Faces* (1938).

right
The way the gangsters liked to go out, or at least the way the Hays Code liked them to. James Cagney about to depart in a sheet of flame in *White Heat* (1949).

Dana Andrews has the chance to compare the portrait, which he admires, with the real Gene Tierney, whom he comes to love, in Otto Preminger's *Laura* (1944).

as a detective. It was a predicament he found himself in again in *Where the Sidewalk Ends* (1950). As a detective, he kills a suspect, falls in love with the widow, and tries to engineer his own death to expose a criminal.

The semi-documentary film which purports to be 'just one of the cases from the files of the Homicide Department' had a vogue in the 1940s. It reached its apogee in *The Naked City* (1948), in which 'New York City and its people were photographed in actual settings'. More interesting of the realistic films were *Double Indemnity* (1944), which had Fred MacMurray as an insurance investigator persuaded by Barbara Stanwyck to commit murder to collect the insurance, and *Call Northside 777* (1948), in which James Stewart as a reporter saves an innocent man from a murder charge.

Occupied postwar Vienna was the setting for *The Third Man* (1949), Carol Reed's direction of Graham Greene's story. A complex plot, good cast, genuine mystery, haunting music and fine atmosphere made the film a

Jean-Paul Belmondo has established himself as a gangster in modern French films. In *The Burglars* (1971) he is chased by Omar Sharif and dodges from buses to cars and back.

classic. Graham Greene was also associated with one of the best crime films made in Britain, *Brighton Rock* (1947), where Richard Attenborough was effective as the leader of a Brighton racecourse gang.

Professionalism was the theme of *This Gun For Hire* (1942), from another Graham Greene story. Alan Ladd played a hired gun with a skill and lack of expression which made him a star. *The Killers* (1954) also featured hired guns (Lee Marvin and Clu Gulager) who chill with the ruthless and business-like way with which they fulfil their contract in a school for blind people. Robbery was committed with style and professionalism in Jules Dassin's *Rififi* (1955). The film was notable for a twenty-minute silent sequence in which the robbery took place, with the aid of an umbrella stuck through a hole drilled in a floor and then opened to prevent rubble falling to the floor below as the hole was enlarged.

Suspense films, of course, often feature crime. Hitchcock is the acknowledged master. In *The Man Who Knew Too Much* (1956), Hitchcock, too, dispensed with dialogue for several minutes as we await a crash of cymbals at a concert, knowing a shooting has been arranged to coincide with it. In *Rear Window* (1954), much of the action is seen from the point of view of James Stewart, a photographer with a broken leg, who, spying on the apartments opposite his window, witnesses a murder. Hitchcock achieves suspense by having the audience, with Stewart, watch Grace Kelly in the murderer's room while the murderer, unknown to her, is outside the door.

As the crime film of the 1930s mirrored the activities of the mobs, so in the 1950s the films expressed contemporary problems. The motorcycle-gang movie began with Marlon Brando and Lee Marvin in *The Wild One* (1954), and had many inferior imitators. James Dean became the *Rebel Without a Cause* (1955), and classroom revolt and violence led to *The Blackboard Jungle* in the same year. Corruption in unions was the subject of Elia Kazan's *On the Waterfront* (1954), where Marlon Brando, a failed boxer, defied the gangster leader of the docker's union, the terrifying Lee J. Cobb, and was badly beaten up for his pains.

Violence has always been part of the crime film, and Brando received another battering as a sheriff in *The Chase* (1965). Early gangster films tended to shun gruesome scenes of violence: guns would crack, bodies

far left
Orson Welles as Harry Lime at bay in the sewers in *The Third Man* (1949).

above
Richard Attenborough trys to persuade his young waitress wife Carol Marsh to commit suicide in *Brighton Rock* (1947), as the sound of police footsteps on the pier above add to their terror.

left
Alan Ladd as the hired gun in *This Gun For Hire* (1942), with Veronica Lake, who became his best-known leading lady.

Lee J. Cobb, the corrupt dockers'
leader, and Marlon Brando, the rebel
docker, being kept apart in *On the
Waterfront* (1954).

would slump, fists would smack into faces, but we were not shown entrails or sophisticated torture. Alan Ladd took a nice beating in *The Glass Key* (1942), but it was after the Second World War that violence in films escalated. In *The Big Heat* (1953) Lee Marvin threw a flaskful of boiling coffee into Gloria Grahame's face – a big step from Cagney's half grapefruit to Mae Clarke's face 22 years earlier. The cops, too, began to get violent. Richard Widmark as *Madigan* (1968), a New York detective, and Clint Eastwood as a plain-clothes policeman in *Dirty Harry* (1971) were as brutal in their methods as the criminals.

By 1973 in *Gordon's War*, Paul Winfield concluded a beating-up by propping his victim's heels on a box and stamping on his legs. Jack Nicholson in *Chinatown* (1974) had his nose slit with a knife. In *The New Centurions* (1972) we see viscera and a baby battering, and George C. Scott, a cop, shoots himself in the mouth.

Nor is violence excluded from those films which look back on the real criminals of the American gangster era. *Bonnie and Clyde* (1967) had Warren Beatty and Faye Dunaway as the itinerant robbers, and the wounds they inflicted on their flight from bank to bank were graphically shown.

The bystanders on the sidewalk show a healthy respect for Clint Eastwood and his gun in *Dirty Harry* (1971).

After the lives of the big-time gangsters, *Dillinger* (1945), *Baby Face Nelson* (1957), *The Rise and Fall of Legs Diamond* (1960), *Al Capone* (1965) – and a study of the biggest event in gangsterdom, *The St. Valentine's Day Massacre* (1967), film-makers turned to current revelations about the Mafia and drug-trafficking for their themes. The first big-budget film about the Mafia, Martin Ritt's *The Brotherhood* (1968) lacked authenticity, and was a flop at the box-office. Nevertheless a novel by Mario Puzo led to one of the most publicized and successful crime films, Francis Ford Coppola's *The Godfather* (1971), with Marlon Brando in the name part as the head of a Mafia-type organization. The film is a self-conscious block-buster, which leads to over-elaboration and a fussy attention to detail, making the action slow. Although the now obligatory violence is present, the film manages to be tedious. Joseph Valachi's revelations of Mafia activity in a series of televised confessions were the subject of *The Valachi Papers* (1972), but the film was badly directed. Better was *Honor Thy Father* (1973), based on Guy Talese's book, but the Mafia film is not likely to become an outstanding sub-genre.

A drug-trafficking scandal inspired William Friedkin's *The French Connection* (1971), in which the real cop in the case had a part alongside Gene Hackman, who played him. The film includes one of the best-ever chase

left
Warren Beatty and Faye Dunaway shoot
it out from behind their car in Arthur
Penn's *Bonnie and Clyde* (1967).

above
Plain-clothes (?) detectives Gene
Hackman and Roy Scheider in *The
French Connection* (1971) frisk Alan
Weeks, a suspected drug-pusher.

Edward G. Robinson and Eli Wallach
used a wheelchair as a prop in their plan
to rob a casino in *Seven Thieves* (1960).
Sebastian Cabot is the unsuspecting
casino official.

above
Stacy Keach as a policeman in *The
New Centurions* (1972), known as
Precinct 45 in Great Britain.

right
Marlon Brando as *The Godfather* (1971)
with Al Pacino as his heir-apparent.

sequences, with a car at ground level
pursuing a train on an elevated track.

Better prospects face the movie in
which sympathetic crooks fail to profit
from their crimes and escape retribu-
tion. The best of these so far is *Seven
Thieves* (1960), in which the accom-
plices cleverly rob a casino, only to
have a change of heart when their
leader (Edward G. Robinson again)
dies, which causes them surreptitiously
to return the money. Steve McQueen
actually did get away with the spoils in
The Getaway (1972) for no other reason
than that his bank robber was the most
likeable character in the film. Walter
Matthau robs a bank in Don Siegel's
Charley Varrick (1973), and as the
money is the Mafia's, he is pursued by
the mob as well as the police. His
accomplice (Andy Robinson) is elim-
inated by the Mafia's heavy in a
particularly bloody scene (crime still
doesn't pay for some), but Matthau
escapes with the loot. The criminals
have finally bumped off the Hays Code.

The Hollywood Musical

Another opening, another show

The title song from *Broadway Melody* (1929). Anita Page (*left*) and Bessie Love partner Charles King. The girls play sisters who both fall in love with King.

Musicals needed sound, but, and maybe a lot less obviously, it worked the other way too – at least at first. Early sound-recording was full of snags. The mikes picked up every noise – our heroine tripping gaily on to the sound stage came across like a herd of buffalo, and beaded dresses were out (unless they were very tight). Volume control was yet another headache. So when Al Jolson flung wide his arms and sang out his love and devotion to his Mammy in *The Jazz Singer* in 1927, Warners were at least cutting their problems down to a minimum; while the actors were singing, the mikes couldn't go picking up extraneous sound.

Of course everyone jumped on the band wagon. Silents were recalled and given a musical score; no film was complete without its theme song; and the musical world was ransacked for talent and ideas. John Boles, Jack Buchanan, Eddie Cantor, Maurice Chevalier, Fanny Brice, Jeanette Mac-Donald, and Sophie Tucker – they were all roped in, while the list of Broadway hits rapidly made over for the screen grew longer: *Rio Rita*

above
Scantily dressed girls and extravagant
sets were both part of the splendour
that was Berkeley. The 'Spin a little web
of dreams' sequence from *Fashions of
1934*.

right
Paul Whiteman and his band in a
number from *The King of Jazz* (1930).

(1929), *The Desert Song* (1929), *Show-boat* (1929), *Viennese Nights* (1930),
and so on. But Hollywood had its own
ideas too. There was *Broadway Melody*
(1929) and the back-stage story – a
natural for endless dance routines and
permutations on the chorine-wins-
big-break-and-leading-man situation.
Ruby Keeler and Dick Powell would
get a lot of mileage out of that one in
the mid 1930s. All-star revue came
over bigger initially. MGM's *Holly-wood Revue* (1929) was the first; then
there were Warners' *Show of Shows*
(1929), *Paramount on Parade* (1930),
and Universal's *The King of Jazz*
(1930), each one more spectacular
than the last. Buster Keaton in an

below
Fred Astaire and Ginger Rogers in *Top Hat* (1935). Said a critic, '. . . watching him, you are suddenly aware that the lower half of the screen has been wasted all these years.'

right
The girls: stand-by of many a musical.

bottom
Operetta from Nelson Eddy and Jeanette MacDonald in *Maytime* (1937).

GEORG

~with **ALICE FA**
JAMES DU

underwater hootchy-kootchy, John Barrymore doing his Richard III, or 500 cowboys galloping out of the ocean – you could never be sure what you'd see next. And then, quite suddenly, the public was bored. The film musical died the first of its several 'deaths', and by the end of 1930 impressarios were billing their talkies as positively NOT musicals.

But by 1933 the musical was on the up again. Two men whose names

WHITE'S 1935 SCANDALS

NED SPARKS · BENNY RUBIN · EMMA DUNN
LYDA ROBERTI · CLIFF EDWARDS · GEORGE WHITE
ARLINE JUDGE · ELEANOR POWELL

Copyright MCMXXXV Fox Film Corp. This display is the property of the Fox Film Corp. It is leased not sold and must be returned to the Fox Film Exchange. Made in U. S. A

would be synonymous with 1930s style were making the big time. They were, of course, Fred Astaire and Busby Berkeley.

Berkeley got his chance when Darryl F. Zanuck, then studio manager at Warners, hired him to choreograph *42nd Street* (1933). It was the start of a series of utterly cinematic extravaganzas, a complete break from the stage-bound conventions of the first phase, and it included *The Gold Diggers of 1933*, *Footlight Parade* (1933), *Fashions of 1934*, *Dames* (1934), *Wonder Bar* (1934), *Gold Diggers of 1935*, *Stars over Broadway* (1935), and so on until in 1939 Warners tried to cut his spending and he left, for MGM. Berkeley's imitators were legion, but they seized on the incidentals – the vast sets, the masses of girls – and lost the heart of his work entirely. It was the camera that danced through his set pieces. Above, below, between the girls it moved, while the geometrical patterns formed, dissolved, and reformed. A hundred girls sliding down a waterfall into a forest lake (*Footlight Parade*), fifty lolling on piano stools while their instruments danced (*Gold Diggers of 1935*) – scenes like this became the surreal images of a strangely impersonal delight.

With Astaire it was different. The camera didn't dominate; it aided and abetted while Fred and Ginger stole

below
The first musical to come out of Arthur Freed's production unit at MGM. Ray Bolger played the scarecrow Judy Garland meets on her way to see *The Wizard of Oz* (1939).

right
Shirley Temple and Bill Robinson stepping it out in *The Little Colonel* (1935), made the year she became top box-office draw.

hearts away. The partnership began with *Flying Down to Rio* (1933) and Astaire and Rogers doing a speciality dance called the Carioca. It lasted six years and produced some marvellous films, amongst them *Top Hat* (1935), *The Gay Divorcée* (1934), *Swing Time* (1936), and *Carefree* (1938). Astaire had later and greater partners, but neither Hayworth nor Charisse are remembered the way Rogers is. 'He gives her class,' said Katharine Hepburn, 'and she gives him sex.' But, though you knew they were meant for each other, there was always a surface edginess in their relationship to keep things interesting.

Only in the last reel would Ginger surrender to Astaire's outright romanticism. He got solo spots in most of the films too, and took your breath away with the sheer inventiveness of a sequence like the musical golf number in *Carefree* or his light, easy way with songs like 'I won't dance' or 'Pick yourself up'.

The other big star partnership of the 1930s was a singing duo, Jeanette MacDonald and Nelson Eddy. Jeanette had already done a number of musicals, notably Ernst Lubitsch's *The Love Parade* (1929), *Monte Carlo* (1930), and *The Merry Widow* (1934), but it was the teaming that began in

1935 with *Naughty Marietta* which really made her name. They were a curious pair: she had all the charm, and a flicker of humour that saw her through some unlikely plotting; he never quite stopped looking like the stand-in. They were a throwback to the romantic world of Viennese operetta and their days were numbered. Still, for a while they made music at the box-office and MGM put them into seven more films in the next seven years, among them *Rose Marie* (1936), *Maytime* (1937), and *Bitter Sweet* (1940).

There were, of course, other stars and other musicals. The 1930s were

vintage years for child performers. The biggest was Shirley Temple; singing, tap-dancing, and generally getting everyone organized, she was voted the world's top box-office attraction five years running, and the memory of songs like 'On the good ship Lollipop' and 'Animal crackers in my soup' seems hardly to have faded at all. Then there was Deanna Durbin, the teenage soprano who made a big hit in *Three Smart Girls* (1937), her first for Universal, where she stayed till 1949 when she announced she was 'tired of playing little girls'. And MGM's Judy Garland, romantically teamed with Mickey Rooney in a succession of I-know-everybody-let's-put-on-a-show movies and seizing her first great part, Dorothy, in *The Wizard of Oz* in 1939. In the senior league came Bing Crosby, relaxed, casual, like he was pacing himself for an apparently effortless jog

through nigh on twenty-five years of musical stardom; John Boles, the gentle tenor who supplied the male interest in some of the early operettas; Maurice Chevalier, quickly wearing out his welcome as the risqué boulevardier; Grace Moore, most successful of the opera stars who tried their luck in films; warm, soft, Alice Faye; and Irene Dunne, who played in the best of Hollywood's three versions of *Showboat* (1936).

In 1939 songwriter Arthur Freed turned producer. It was an important move for he immediately began collecting talent around him at MGM. What he offered was space, room to expand and experiment while he took care of the front office. The policy paid off: directors came, attracted by the freedom; so did songwriters and costume designers. And the result was the most brilliant series of musicals so far made. But they weren't just good;

left
Ballet = Fantasy in the 'Day in New York' sequence from *On the Town* (1949). Kelly is remembering Miss Turnstiles alias Vera-Ellen, the girl he met earlier in his 24-hour furlough.

IRE ★ *Eleanor* POWELL

"When they begin the Beguine"... greatest of all dancing thrills.

DWAY MELODY *of* 1940

above
Eleanor Powell was in all three
Broadway Melody reprises (the others
were '36 and '38). They were star
vehicles, built around her brilliant tap.
This one had Astaire of course (he and
Rogers had just split) and songs by Cole
Porter.

they were different from almost every-thing that had come before. Only the earlier work of Lubitsch and Rouben Mamoulian had the same integrated quality, the same sense of dance and song springing naturally from drama-tic action and emotion. These weren't flimsy star vehicles; they were musical dramas. Vincente Minnelli, Stanley Donen, and Gene Kelly were probably Freed's biggest finds. Minnelli came from Broadway and had a string of designer/directors jobs behind him already. *Meet Me in St Louis* (1944) was his second full director credit and a deceptively simple bit of Americana with Garland giving a performance of touching innocence which finds its high point in 'Have yourself a merry little Christmas'. *An American in Paris* (1951) was less coherent – Gene Kelly's choreography ran away with him in the ballet; but *The Band Wagon* (1953) worked splendidly, putting Astaire back on top after a lull in his career and giving him an exciting new part-ner, Cyd Charisse. Donen and Kelly collaborated on two of the great MGM musicals: *On the Town* (1949) and *Singin' in the Rain* (1952). The title number in the latter is Kelly, but there are so many good things in them both – 'New York, New York' and the title number from *On the Town*; the 'Broadway Ballet', 'You were meant for me', and the Berkeley pas-tiches from *Singin' in the Rain* – that it's hard to choose a favourite. Alone, Donen later made *Seven Brides for Seven Brothers* (1954), which also rates fairly high marks. Choreographer turned director Charles Walters had some good credits too, among them *Easter Parade* (1948), with Astaire and Garland in a Pygmalion plot, and *Lili* (1953). And twice Freed tempted Mamoulian back to the musical film; the result, two uniquely imaginative movies, *Summer Holiday* (1946) and *Silk Stockings* (1956), Astaire's second paring with Cyd Charisse. Freed's wasn't the only musical unit working

left
Gene Kelly *Singin' in the Rain* (1952).

top right
The Mickey Spillane spoof ballet from *The Band Wagon* (1953). Cyd Charisse plays the beautiful girl, Fred Astaire the private eye.

right
The birth of a standard. Judy Garland sings 'The man that got away' from *A Star is Born* (1954). The lyrics were Ira Gershwin, and Harold Arlen wrote the music.

at Metro. Joe Pasternak was given the
job of producing old-style vehicles for
some of the studio's second-liners,
among them Esther Williams, Kath-
ryn Grayson, Howard Keel, and the
Italian tenor Mario Lanza.

The great musicals at MGM may
have been directors' films, but the
studio's brightest stars shone the more
brightly for it. Garland's real gift lay
in her ability to relate in simple,
emotional terms to her audience, and
the new musicals gave her chances
almost entirely lacking in the Rooney-
Garland formula, chances that she
realized most powerfully in her comeback film for Warners, *A Star is Born*
(1954). Kelly, straddling the roles of
dancer, singer, choreographer, and
co-director, had time to develop his
interest in pseudo-classical ballet from

the 'Slaughter on Tenth Avenue'
sequence in *Words and Music* (1948)
to *An American in Paris, Singin' in the
Rain*, and *Invitation to the Dance*
(1954). Still, then and now the public
mostly prefer him as the all-American
good guy, the supreme athlete of the
dance, romancing a mop in *Thousands
Cheer* (1943) or partnering Tom and
Jerry in *Anchors Aweigh* (1944). Astaire
survived gloriously into the new era,
each role, each partner revealing fresh
resources. The MGM years saw his
most imaginative solo work, but he
also handled a complete switch in style
for the ritualized 'Limehouse Blues'
sequence in *The Ziegfeld Follies* (1944)
and turned in a couple of excellent
comedy routines, 'We're a couple of
swells' in *Easter Parade* and 'Triplets'
in *The Band Wagon*.

left
Nun-turned-governess Julie Andrews sings to the little von Trapps. The star and the setting (the Austrian Alps) clicked, and *The Sound of Music* (1965) became the biggest musical money-maker ever.

below
Audrey Hepburn seeing Life in Stanley Donen's *Funny Face* (1956). Fred Astaire played the fashion photographer who went with her to Paris.

right
It was thirteen down and seventeen more to go when Elvis made this one, *Viva Las Vegas*, in 1964. Co-star Ann-Margret didn't repeat the experience.

Elsewhere the mixture was a lot thinner. Fox pushed Betty Grable and Carmen Miranda. Warners had a warm, breathless girl-next-door called Doris Day and a very profitable line in musical biopics, among them *Yankee Doodle Dandy* (1942), *Night and Day* (1945), and *I'll See You in My Dreams* (1951). Hayworth was queen of the Columbia lot and they bought her some classy partners, Astaire in *You'll Never Get Rich* (1941) and *You Were Never Lovelier* (1942) and Kelly in *Cover Girl* (1944). Crosby was still at Paramount and Betty Hutton joined him there.

By the middle of the 1950s the pace was slowing. Television with its everlasting variety shows was the big enemy. Studios forced to cut costs began letting contracts run down, and by 1954 no musical stars were being introduced. Those who survived – people like Day, Sinatra, and Debbie Reynolds – did so because they'd extended their range to comedy and drama. By 1960 confidence was very low: the musical was dying, was dead. Studios needed assurance before they'd venture cash in the field, and they

found it where they'd found it before –
in the cast-iron success of the Broadway hit. The trend had begun in the
late 1950s, with the success of the
Rodgers and Hammerstein series.
West Side Story (1961), *Gypsy* (1962),
My Fair Lady (1964), *The Sound of
Music* (1965), *Camelot* (1967), *Oliver!*
(1968), *Sweet Charity* (1968), *Funny
Girl* (1968), *Hello Dolly!* (1969),
Cabaret (1972): the list of successors
is long, and too often it's been a case
of big films, big stars, and precious
little joy. Of course, there've been
pluses – stars like Julie Andrews, Barbra Streisand, and Liza Minnelli, and
a choreographer of real individuality
in Bob Fosse – so maybe we should
just hold our thumbs and wait. After
all, the musical has been certified dead
before.

Social Concern

The first appearance of the strike-breakers in Eisenstein's *Strike* (1924).

Moving pictures got their first public showings in the penny arcades and the vaudeville theatres. They made you laugh, they made you cry, they told you stories; they did anything but make you think. They were entertainment. Cinema as dream factory has always made commercial sense. The last thing totalitarian government or big financiers want is change – the *status quo* keeps them where they want to be.

It's not surprising then to find few examples of a coherent social policy at work in the history of the cinema. A Swedish company, Svenska Bio, was one such. Charles Magnusson was its guiding force, and in 1912 he signed Victor Sjöström, whose *Ingeborg Holm* (1913), about the poor-law system, quickly showed he was in sympathy with the approach. The American Warner Brothers were another. In the 1930s they put out a series of punchy dramas with a liberal social conscience; the message came straight, as in Mervyn Le Roy's *I Am a Fugitive from a Chain Gang* (1932) with prison brutality taking the rap, or dressed up as biography in William Dieterle's *The Life of Emile Zola* (1937). And at the same time in Great Britain John

Grierson's documentary unit at the Empire Marketing Board (and later the General Post Office) was making films that had a 'social use'; among the most memorable was Elton and Anstey's *Housing Problems* (1935).

Of course the Russians recognized the film's power as an instrument of social change: said Lenin, 'The cinema is for us the most important of the arts.' For a while it even went mobile in propaganda trains – the Cuban socialist revolution of 1959 would pursue a very similar approach – but in Russia what began as a lively, inventive response to a revolutionary situation petered out in the arid stereotypes of Stalinist social realism. The uneven brilliance of the early Eisenstein *Strike* (1924), agit-prop about industrial action brutally suppressed, belongs to the first period.

Elsewhere achievement was piecemeal before the outbreak of the Second World War. Italy and India thrived

right
I Am a Fugitive from a Chain Gang (1932), an exposé of conditions in U.S. prison camps. Paul Muni at the tender mercy of David Landau.

below
Mob rule was the subject under attack in Fritz Lang's first Hollywood film, *Fury* (1936).

Other Hollywood directors with a social conscience included D. W. Griffith (*The Mother and the Law*, 1914, and *Isn't Life Wonderful?* 1924), King Vidor (*Our Daily Bread*, 1934, and *The Crowd*, 1928), Frank Capra (*Mr Smith Goes to Washington*, 1939) and John Ford (*The Grapes of Wrath*, 1940, and *Tobacco Road*, 1941). For a short space in the 1930s it looked like consciences paid off the only way Hollywood understood. But for all their attacks on poverty and corruption all these post-Depression movies were often hopelessly compromised, forced by the entertainment ethic to play up what they sought to condemn.

Spain's Luis Buñuel, working in the French avant-garde, produced two savage attacks on the way society represses sexuality, *Un Chien Andalou* (1928) and *L'Age d'Or* (1930); later he returned to Spain for the documentary *Tierra sin Pan* (1932), about poverty amongst the Hurdes. France, like Italy, demonstrated a trend towards realism very early, but of overt social criticism there was little before Jean Vigo's blistering attacks on the idle rich, *A Propos de Nice* (1930), and repressive education, *Zéro de Conduite* (1934). Renoir's approach was basically much more diffuse, although *La Règle du Jeu* (1939) gives a clear account of a corrupt society bent on destroying itself.

After the Second World War Germany produced a significantly large quota of films dealing with post-war adjustment. It would be easy to dismiss the phenomenon as evidence of the 'trauma' of defeat. One should remember, however, that the British and Americans kept a tight control on subject matter in occupied territories. Important German names included directors Wolfgang Staudte, Gerhard Lamprecht, Helmut Käutner, and Robert Stemmle, and the causes and effects of Nazism were still being debated in the early 1960s. In Japan the immediate post-war period saw a shift towards social realism, with the geisha system a frequent theme (not surprisingly since the new constitution gave women the vote). More recently Nagisa Oshima, leader of Japan's 'new wave', has begun making politically-aware social dramas like *Death by Hanging* (1968) and *The Ceremony* (1970), an attack on bourgeois traditions.

Oshima has occasionally been influenced by Jean-Luc Godard, France's strongest social critic. Increasingly his political beliefs draw him away from the commercial cinema,

on a diet of spectaculars; but India did produce a handful of films dealing, albeit romantically, with the caste system, among them Chandra Barua's *Devdas* (1935) and Himansu Rai's *Untouchable Girl* (1936), and in Italy Alessandro Blasetti made *Sun* (1929), on the effects of reclamation in the marshes south of Rome. The focus of German cinema in the 1920s and early 1930s was psychological rather than social, with director Fritz Lang a rare exception. The oversimplifications of *Metropolis* (1926) are hard to take: he seems to be proposing emotion as the cure-all in labour relations. But in *M* (1931) he debates the relationship between justice and law, a theme he treated even more explicitly in his American social trilogy, *Fury* (1936), *You Only Live Once* (1937), and *You and Me* (1938).

Mental breakdown is the theme of *The Snake Pit* (1948), starring Olivia de Havilland (*centre*). Criticized by some for its sensationalism, the film did alert the American public to the overcrowding in mental hospitals.

and *Masculin-Feminin* (1965), *Deux ou Trois Choses que je Sais d'Elle* (1966), and *Weekend* (1967) mark some of the stages in that development. Other notable post-war work includes André Cayatte's judicial series, pillorying the legal system; Claude Autant-Lara's attacks on the Church, military, and bourgeoisie; Alain Resnais's *Hiroshima Mon Amour* (1959); and Louis Malle's Indian documentaries.

In Italy Roberto Rossellini's *Rome, Open City* (1945) signalled the birth of neo-realism. Alongside the actuality and deliberate simplification of style was an implicit left-wing commitment, which found expression in a variety of topical themes such as crime and corruption (Alberto Lattuada's *Il Bandito*, 1946, and *Senza Pietà*, 1948), the peasant and the South (Guiseppe de Santis' *Non cé Pace tra gli Ulivi*, 1949, and Pietro Germi's *Il Cammino della Speranza*, 1950), and the problems of urban living in post-war Italy (Vittorio de Sica's *Bicycle Thieves*, 1948, and *Umberto D*, 1952). By 1951 the impetus had gone and since then only the work of Michelangelo Antonioni has revealed a consistent social concern, although stylistically the effects of neo-realism were much longer lasting. Federico Fellini's *La Dolce Vita* (1959), Luchino Visconti's *Rocco*

top right
Frank Sinatra played the junkie in
Preminger's *The Man with a Golden
Arm* (1956).

right
Ken Loach's *Family Life* (1971), a
moving demonstration of the theory that
environment is the true cause of mental
illness. Sandy Ratcliff plays the girl who
retreats into schizophrenia; Bill Dean
and Grace Cave her parents.

The marathon dances of the 1930s become a metaphor for Depression America in *They Shoot Horses, Don't They?* (1969).

and His Brothers (1960), and Pier Paolo Pasolini's *Accatone* (1961) were, however, significant statements about modern Italian society.

American cinema also struck a vein of realism in the immediate post-war period. Social themes such as the adjustment to peace (*The Best Years of Our Lives*, 1946, and *The Men*, 1950) and racialism (*Gentleman's Agreement*, 1947, *Crossfire*, 1947, and *Intruder in the Dust*, 1949) were honestly treated. But by the early 1950s Senator McCarthy had contrived to make the charge of liberalism a dangerous one and, with films like *The Best Years of Our Lives* being investigated, Hollywood began to tread a lot more carefully. Director Otto Preminger was one of the first to tackle the 'strong' subject again, but there was more than a little showmanship in his

approach to films like *The Man with the Golden Arm* (1956). Important films of the period included *On the Waterfront* (1954), *The Defiant Ones* (1958), *The Hustler* (1961), and *Dr Strangelove* (1963).

In Britain the commercial cinema was slower to begin making films with a serious social purpose. Initially the movement towards realism was literary and theatrical, but in 1958, with *Room at the Top*, a series of films dealing with the problems of the working-class began, amongst them *Saturday Night and Sunday Morning* (1960), *A Taste of Honey* (1961), and *A Kind of Loving* (1962). Ken Loach is the most committed film-maker to have emerged since, *Kes* (1969) and *Family Life* (1971) both examining areas of deprivation in contemporary British society.

Animation

Making a dinosaur move

Animated films are those which give movement and life to objects which are still, such as drawings or puppets. The effect is achieved by exposing one frame of film at a time, adjusting the drawing or puppet between exposures. The technique is called stop-frame cinematography, and the rapid projection of the succession of pictures gives the illusion of coherent movement. Animation, in fact, preceded motion pictures, as a succession of drawings rapidly cranked through a magic lantern gives a crude effect of movement.

Emile Cohl, a Frenchman, made the first film cartoon series in 1908 with the adventures of a little man, simply drawn in white in a black frame. Soon afterwards Winsor McKay in America made the delightful *Gertie the Trained Dinosaur* (1909), using 10,000 drawings, and later he made the first serious cartoon, *The Sinking of the Lusitania* (1918). In the 1920s cartoon characters like Max Fleischer's Betty Boop and Pat Sullivan's Felix the Cat were very popular, despite the necessary shortness of the films. Increased action was imparted

Mickey Mouse in 'The Sorcerer's Apprentice' sequence in Disney's *Fantasia* (1940).

to them by the carefully synchronized music of the resident theatre pianist. The coming of sound gave a valuable extra dimension to the cartoon film, enabling the producer to control the whole effect. It was used successfully in a number of experimental films made in Europe, principally in Germany, France and Britain, where Len Lye used abstract patterns to give a visual interpretation to popular music.

137

Silhouettes or puppets were used by the best European animators: Lotte Reiniger in Germany, Berthold Bartosch in France and George Pal in Holland.

Walt Disney in America became the most successful of the film animators. He produced his first Mickey Mouse cartoon *Steamboat Willie* in 1928, at the beginning of the sound era, and gave up drawing to supervise a studio which added Donald Duck and Pluto to Mickey as world-famous characters. Disney was not without rivals. Max Fleischer in 1933 began his popular Popeye series of over 250 shorts and Tex Avery in 1937 created Tom and Jerry, the cat and mouse adversaries whose inventive and much criticized violence towards each other is equalled by their capacity to survive it. Their award-winning shorts are still popular on television.

above
Gertie the Trained Dinosaur (1909), Winsor McKay's early cartoon character.

right
Britain's first full-length cartoon feature. Halas and Batchelor's *Animal Farm* (1954).

top right
Jerry and partner face Tom in the Oscar-winning cartoon *Two Mouse-keteers* (1951).

Disney's golden period came with a series of full-length features, beginning with *Snow White and the Seven Dwarfs* (1937). *Fantasia* (1940) was eight cartoon pieces set to classical music. One piece, Mussorgsky's 'Night on a Bare Mountain' had been the subject and title of a French cartoon in 1934. *Dumbo* (1941) an elephant, and *Bambi* (1943), a deer, were very

right
Gorilla's Dance (1969), from Zagreb
Film of Yugoslavia, directed by Milan
Blažeković, with screenplay by Dušan
Vukotić.

below
George Dunning's *Yellow Submarine*
(1968), the full-length Beatles film:
John Lennon (*right*) and George
Harrison (*centre*).

successful, but after these Disney's main work was concerned with good, if sentimental, nature films. *Mary Poppins* (1964), however, combined real actors with animated drawings.

United Productions of America (UPA) was founded by a breakaway group from Disney in 1945, and their Mr Magoo is a well known cartoon character. John Halas and Joy Batchelor have made cartoons in Great Britain since 1936, including Britain's first full-length feature, Orwell's *Animal Farm* (1954). Eastern Europe has developed a tradition for animation, particularly Poland (some of whose

best film-makers eventually joined the French movement), Czechoslovakia, with Jiři Trnka and Karel Zeman, and Yugoslavia, with Dušan Vukotić and others at the Zagreb Studios. Norman McLaren, who went from Britain to Canada in 1941 to inspire a school of animation, consistently refined technique and made a fine film *Pas de Deux* (1968) using multiple images of the movements of two dancers. A Canadian animator, George Dunning, returned the compliment by moving to Britain in the 1950s and making the full-length cartoon film of the Beatles, *The Yellow Submarine* (1968).

Disney's first full-length cartoon, *Snow White and the Seven Dwarfs* (1938) won eight Academy Awards, and was immensely popular.

141

The French Cinema

A few French names – Lumière, Méliès, Leon Gaumont, Charles Pathé – indicate the dominance of France in pioneering the film industry, and the French contribution to films has remained second only to that of the U.S.A.

Abel Gance began a tradition of great long-living French directors with *J'Accuse* (1919) and *Napoléon* (1927), and produced films till the 1970s. René Clair, who wrote his own screenplays, developed a vein of sophisticated comedy with *Un Chapeau de Paille d'Italie* (1927) and *Sous les Toits de Paris* (1930). Avant-garde experimental films were made by Jean Cocteau (*Le Sang d'un Poète*, 1930) and Luis Buñuel (*Un Chien Andalou*, 1928, with Salvador Dali). Cocteau's masterpiece was *Orphée* (1950) and Buñuel made

Henri Serre and Oskar Werner are friends who both love Jeanne Moreau in *Jules et Jim* (1961), from an old novel by Henri-Pierre Roche which has been rediscovered by a new generation of readers.

Belle de Jour (1967). Buñuel is a Spaniard, whose best films were made in France, as were those of Carl Dreyer, a Dane, who made *Le Passion de Jeanne d'Arc* (1928) and one of the best horror films, *Vampyr* (1932). German directors G. W. Pabst, Fritz Lang and Max Ophüls also worked in France, the last-named making the comedy of love's merry-go-round, *La Ronde* (1950). Jean Renoir made good films for 45 years, including *La Grande Illusion* (1936) and *La Règle du Jeu* (1939), the first starring Jean Gabin, France's best-known actor. Just before the Second World War, other French directors were making their mark. Julien Duvivier made *Un Carnet de Bal* (1937) and afterwards made the series of Don Camillo comedies, which made an international name for Fernandel. Marcel Carné made the very funny *Drôle de Drame* (1937), with a cast of stars including Louis Jouvet

and Jean-Louis Barrault, and *Le Jour se Lève* (1939) with Jean Gabin and Michèle Morgan. After the war he made one of the classics of the cinema, *Les Enfants du Paradis* (1944), with Arletty giving a memorable performance. All three films were scripted by Jacques Prévert.

Robert Bresson used non-professional actors, his masterpiece perhaps being *Un Condamné à Mort s'est Échappé* (1956).

A new wave of French directors made post-war films alongside the old guard. Jean-Luc Godard was the most influential. His first feature, *A Bout de Souffle* starred Jean-Paul Belmondo and Jean Seberg, and his

above
Charles Vanel and Yves Montand as long-distance lorry drivers with an explosive load in *Le Salaire de la Peur* (*The Wages of Fear*, 1952), directed by Henri-Georges Clouzot.

right
Jean Gabin with Arletty at the bar in Marcel Carné's *Le Jour se Lève* (1939).

subsequent output, including *Alphaville* (1965) and *Weekend* (1967), was prolific, varied and brilliant. Louis Malle made *Les Amants* (1958) with Moreau, *Vie Privée* (1961) with Bardot and *Viva Maria!* (1965) with both. François Truffaut also starred Moreau in the beautiful *Jules et Jim* (1961), who love and share her.

Other directors like Louis Feuillade, Sacha Guitry, Jean Vigo, Marcel Pagnol and Jacques Feyder, and performers like Raimu, Maurice Chevalier, Gerard Phillipe, Simone Signoret and the actor-director Jacques Tati emphasize the excellence, past and present, of French cinema.

The Cinema in Britain

Great expectations

above
John Gielgud and Jessie Matthews in the 'Three wishes' number from Victor Saville's *The Good Companions* (1932).

top
Gracie Fields singing along in Basil Dean's *The Show Goes On* (1937).

right
The Royal Ballet star, Moira Shearer, danced in Michael Powell's *The Red Shoes* (1948). Choreography was by Robert Helpmann.

Although many of the technical advances which made the motion picture possible were developed in Great Britain, the British cinema has never been able to build a firm industry on its early efforts. Crisis-ridden almost from its birth, bolstered-up by a government-imposed quota system limiting the number of foreign films shown in British cinemas – a system which may have increased the quantity of film-making in Britain at some periods, but has done nothing for the quality – and staggering from one financial collapse to another, the British cinema's output of feature films has had only two significant phases: the 1940s and the 1960s.

Until the 'New British Cinema' of the 1960s came into being, helped by a comprehensive relaxation of censorship in the arts, the British feature film showed no continuing traditional style or phase. A certain music hall tradition in some British comedy films, particularly the very popular films of George Formby, Gracie Fields, and to a lesser extent, Will Hay, in the 1930s; or the whimsical gaiety of such Jessie Matthews musicals as *The Good Companions* (1932) and *Evergreen* (1934), both directed by Victor Saville, could tentatively be considered British 'styles'. But until the coming of the 'provincial realism' films at the end of the 1950s, there was no British genre to compare with the American Western, musical or crime film. The Ealing Comedy lasted only a decade, while the thrilling suspense style developed by Alfred Hitchcock in such films as *The Lodger* (1926), *Blackmail* (1929), *The Man Who Knew too Much* (1934) and *The Thirty-Nine Steps* (1935) were typically Hitchcock rather than typically British. After *Jamaica Inn* (1939) Hitchcock moved to the United States,

where his British origins had little to do with the steady growth of his reputation as one of the cinema's great directors.

In the 1930s, the surprising international success of Alexander Korda's *The Private Life of Henry VIII* (1933) led many film-makers to the misguided conclusion that the way to financial success was via the international super-production which would be accepted on a par with the output of Hollywood. Some, such as Korda's *Things to Come* (1935) and *Rembrandt* (1936), still look good forty years later. On the whole, however, the results of this policy were pretentious and shallow, and their expense

helped the British film industry to collapse into financial chaos in 1937. English studios had also been over-producing, to grab all the profits they could out of the quota system which was keeping much of the more sophisticated and artistically satisfying product of Hollywood studios out of British cinemas. It was a self-defeating system. The 'quota quickies' of the 1930s were so bad they alienated cinema audiences, and American studios found that it was to their financial benefit to get round the system by making films, with American directors, stars and money, in English studios. MGM-British did have Michael Balcon, the English producer who had

discovered Hitchcock in the 1920s, as its producer, but it was American money and American directors who made *A Yank at Oxford* (1938), which starred Robert Taylor and Vivien Leigh, *Goodbye, Mr Chips* and *The Citadel* (1939), both of which starred the English actor Robert Donat.

But for the outbreak of the Second World War, the British cinema could have seen a familiar situation repeated. With no language barrier to hinder its acceptance in Britain, limitless cash resources, and a much wider vision of the possibilities of the medium, the American film industry had always been one of the major causes of the weakness of the British. But the war

opposite
Charles Frend's *The Foreman Went to France* (1942) was based on the true story of a factory foreman who went to France in 1940 to rescue machinery before the Germans captured it.

right
Fires Were Started (1943) was Humphrey Jennings' account of fire-fighting in the blitz, and used real firemen instead of actors.

below
Laurence Olivier as the King in his film of Shakespeare's *Henry V* (1945).

below
Dennis Price, Alec Guinness and Valerie Hobson in *Kind Hearts and Coronets* (1949).

bottom
Bobby Henrey and Ralph Richardson in Carol Reed's *The Fallen Idol* (1948).

sent the Americans home and caused the over-extended British industry to contract into a new slim-line, more efficient version of itself. War-time conditions brought cinemas a large, enthusiastic and suddenly patriotic audience, ready to welcome the output of the country's own film-makers.

The 'golden age' which followed and which was to last almost to the late 1940s, had a major part of its roots in the documentary movement which throughout the 1930s had been pro-ducing films which looked firmly to Britain and the British way of life for their inspiration and which has been the British film industry's one great contribution to the art of the film. Documentary films were made to provide information: John Grierson's *Drifters* (1929) was about Scotland's herring fleet, Arthur Elton's and Edgar Anstey's *Housing Problems* (1935) was made in the slums of Stepney, London, Paul Rotha's *Shipyard* (1936) was about the building of a ship and the men who built her, Basil Wright's and Harry Watt's *Night Mail* (1935) was made for the General Post Office. These films were not just reportage; they displayed the distinctive point of view of their makers, and their realism and social truth were to have a strong influence on feature film-making.

Michael Balcon had shown his interest in the documentary style in 1934 when he produced Robert Fla-herty's *Man of Aran*, and had injected a documentary-style realism into many

of his 1930s films. In 1938 he took over production at Ealing Studios, a move which turned out to be a milestone in British cinema history.

Not only did Ealing turn out a large number of really fine films from then until the studios closed in the mid-1950s, but it also became the nearest thing Britain had to a film school for many years. Balcon attracted to Ealing a remarkably talented group of film-makers – directors, writers, designers, cameramen, actors and editors – dedi-cated to the creation of films which showed integrity, style and a distinc-tive British character. Among these were *The Foreman Went to France* (1942) and *San Demetrio, London* (1943), both directed by Charles Frend, *Next of Kin* (1942, Thorold Dickin-son), *Nine Men* (1943, Harry Watt), *The Cruel Sea* (1953, Charles Frend), and, of course, that long list of 'Ealing Comedies'. A few of the best: *The Goose Steps Out* (1942) starring Will Hay and directed by Hay and Basil

John Laurie, John Phillips, Norman Wooland and Laurence Olivier in *Richard III* (1955).

Dearden, *Whisky Galore* (1947) the first feature film directed by Alexander Mackendrick, *Kind Hearts and Coro-nets* (1949) directed by Robert Hamer and starring Dennis Price and Alec Guinness in eight roles, *The Lavender Hill Mob* (1951) directed by Charles Crichton and starring Alec Guinness and Stanley Holloway, and *The Lady-*

far right
Rachel Roberts and Albert Finney in
Saturday Night and Sunday Morning
(1960).

right
Sean Connery's James Bond in trouble
again, this time in *Goldfinger* (1964),
directed by Guy Hamilton.

below
Dirk Bogarde and James Fox in Joseph
Losey's *The Servant* (1963).

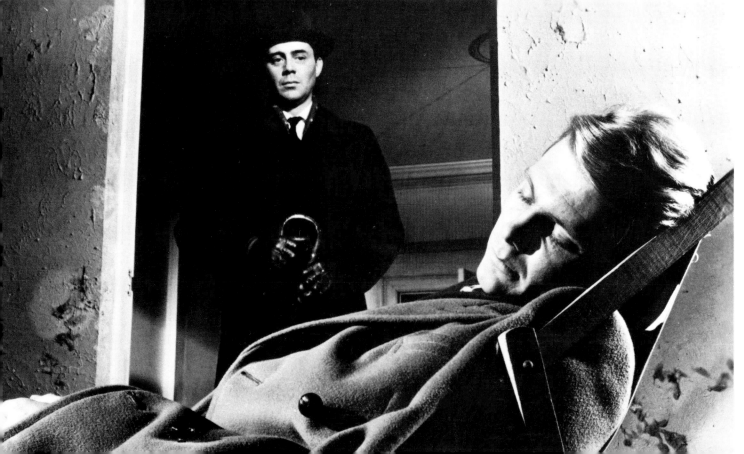

killers (1955) again with Guinness, this time directed by Alexander Mackendrick.

Another man who was to have a big influence in the British cinema, J. Arthur Rank, also came to the fore during the war years. His empire included hundreds of cinemas as well as such production studios as Gainsborough, where those memorable gothic romances, *The Man in Grey* (1943) and *The Wicked Lady* (1945), were made, Two Cities, Independent Producers and Archers. By the war's end, the Rank Organization was the major force in British cinema, J. Arthur Rank following a much more ambitious policy than Balcon at Ealing. As before, the pursuit of the beautiful vision of a British international movie centre was to be disastrous, and the extravagance of such productions as Gabriel Pascal's *Caesar and Cleopatra* (1945) was nearly the downfall of Rank. But it was Rank finance which made possible many good films, including Laurence Oliv-

ier's *Henry V* (1945) and *Hamlet* (1947), *The Red Shoes* (1948), directed by Michael Powell, and many of the best films of directors like David Lean, Carol Reed, Launder and Gilliatt, Powell and others. In its day, the Rank muscle-man beating his gong was as familiar a sight at the beginning of films as MGM's lion or Twentieth Century-Fox's searchlights.

Lean and Reed were two major directors dominating British filmmaking in the war years and after. Like John Baxter's *Love on the Dole* (1941), Reed's *The Stars Look Down* (1939) showed the influence of the documentary style in its concern to portray realistically the problems of ordinary working people. His films of this time included two influential war films, *The Way Ahead* (1943) and *The True Glory* (1945, with Garson Kanin), and *Odd Man Out* (1947), *The Fallen Idol* (1948) and *The Third Man* (1949).

David Lean's major war-time films included *In Which We Serve* (1942) which he co-directed with Noël Coward, *This Happy Breed* (1943), *Blithe Spirit* (1944) and *Brief Encounter* (1945), all of which were Coward stories. In 1946, Lean turned to Dickens for inspiration with *Great Expectations* and, in 1947, *Oliver Twist*.

Documentary film production during the war was extensive, and generally of a very high standard. The Government and the Services sponsored film units, helping to make possible such films as *Target for Tonight* (1941, Harry Watt), *Listen to Britain* (1941, Humphrey Jennings, who also made a feature film in 1943, *Fires Were Started*), *Desert Victory* (1943) and *Western Approaches* (1944, Pat Jackson).

If the Second World War provided the British film industry with its first great impetus, the relaxation of censorship in the arts in Britain from the late 1950s on, gave it its second. The

British cinema used the talents of a new generation of novelists, playwrights and film-makers to show the world that the once-taboo subjects of sex and violence could be box-office successes – no difficulty about that! – but could also be treated honestly and realistically. Jack Clayton's *Room at the Top* (1958), based on John Braine's novel, showed the way, and was soon followed by *Look Back in Anger* (1959) and *The Entertainer* (1960), both directed by Tony Richardson from plays by John Osborne, *Saturday Night and Sunday Morning* (1960) in which Karel Reisz directed the then unknown Albert Finney in an adaptation of Alan Sillitoe's novel, *A Taste of Honey* (1961, Richardson), *A Kind of Loving* (1962, John Schlesinger) and *This Sporting Life* (1963, Lindsay Anderson).

Provincial realism was gritty, but Swinging London was the world centre for all that was biggest, brightest and most pop. The 1960s saw a tidal wave of American money and talent pouring into Britain, on the basis of which some of the best films ever made in the country were produced. Many of these were made by American directors: Joseph Losey's *The Servant* (1963), *Accident* (1967) and *The Go-Between* (1971), for instance, or Stanley Kubrick's *2001 – A Space Odyssey* (1968). Others were the work of European directors such as François Truffaut, Roman Polański and Michelangelo Antonioni. But a large number were by British directors, whose work gave the British film industry world stature: Richard Lester's *A Hard Day's Night* (1965), Tony Richardson's *Tom Jones* (1963), John

Schlesinger's *Darling* (1965), Lindsay Anderson's *If...* (1968), Ken Russell's *Women in Love* (1969), Donald Cammell's and Nicholas Roeg's *Performance* (1970), and many more.

By the early 1970s, the bubble had burst. Most of the Americans had gone home, taking several British directors with them. Too much recent British film-making has been of the James Bond, Hammer Horror and Carry On variety, while few directors, with the exceptions of Lindsay Anderson and, on a smaller and more intimate scale, Ken Loach (*Kes* and *Family Life*), Bill Douglas (*My Childhood* and *My Ain Folk*) and others, make films specifically British in content or outlook.

opposite top
David Bradley in *Kes* (1969), directed by Ken Loach.

opposite bottom
Stephen Archibald in *My Ain Folk* (1974), the second film in Bill Douglas' highly praised trilogy based on his childhood in a Scottish mining village.

above
Shoot-up on Speech Day: Christine Noonan and Malcom McDowell in Lindsay Anderson's *If...* (1968).

The German Cinema

below
F. W. Murnau's *The Last Laugh* (1924), an ironic *kammerspiel* film. Emil Jannings plays the old hotel doorman whose life disintegrates when his uniform is taken away from him.

bottom
Lilian Harvey in Germany's biggest musical success in the first years of sound, *The Congress Dances* (1931).

The 1920s were Germany's golden years. Official recognition of the cinema's role as a wartime propaganda machine and the post-war establishment of the giant UFA studios had created the environment for some of the most original world cinema of the decade. The big guns were directorial – Fritz Lang, F. W. Murnau, G. W. Pabst, Ernst Lubitsch – and much of their work fell within three characteristically German genres – expressionist fantasy, *kammerspiel*, and *neue sachlichheit*. Expressionism, the translation of the mind's activity into visual symbols, had its first and purest representation in Robert Wiene's *The Cabinet of Dr Caligari* (1919); later examples include Murnau's *Nosferatu* (1922), Arthur Robison's *Warning Shadows* (1922), and Lang's *Destiny* (1921) and *Metropolis* (1926). Murnau also worked in *kammerspiel* films – *The Last Laugh* (1924) – a highly structured form (it preserved the three unities) concerned with the psychological effects of social destiny in everyday, contemporary life. *Neue sachlichheit* was social realism with an almost documentary quality; Pabst's *The Joyless Street* (1925) and *Pandora's Box* (1928) are fine examples of the type. There was a fourth, immensely popular genre in the 1920s – vastly ambitious, beautifully photographed historical or legendary subjects like Lang's *The Nibelungen Saga* (1924). Lubitsch had been the first to exploit this desire for spectacle, in *Madame Dubarry* (1919, U.S. title *Passion*) and *Anna Boleyn* (1920).

The post-sound, pre-Hitler period was remarkable only for a small group of liberal statements voicing opposition to authoritarianism and militarism in German society, among them Pabst's *Westfront 1918* (1930) and *Kameradschaft* (1931). In March 1933, with the appointment of Goebbels as Minister of Propaganda and Public Enlightenment, the German film industry became the tool of the Nazis. Outwardly Goebbels' touch was light: direct propaganda was kept to a minimum and high-grade escapist entertainment like Werner Hochbaum's *The Favourite of the Empress* (1936) was the norm. But in reality his control was entire. Desirable films were subsidized; the state held the monopoly on technical equipment; productions were subject to continual censorship; cinemas exhibiting 'healthy' films were exempt from entertainment tax. And it is the propaganda films that are remembered, films like Leni Riefenstahl's hymn to fascism, *Triumph of the Will* (1934), and Franz Hippler's anti-Semite documentary *The Eternal Jew* (1940). Many of the most creative people

working in the German cinema left the country, driven out by the Nazi purge on Jews.

Since the defeat of 1945 and the creation of two separate German states, there has been a natural divergence between the cinemas of East and West Germany. However, in the immediate post-war period both countries produced a number of films which accurately mirrored the contemporary mood; the East's *The Murderers Are Amongst Us* (1946) and the West's *The Ballad of Berlin* (1948) were among the most successful. East Germany then fell victim to the schematic social realism which affected the socialist bloc in the late 1940s and early 1950s, and only the documentary work of Andrew and Annelie Thorndike has made much impression internationally. For almost a generation West German cinema was in the doldrums, though its leading part in the sexploitation boom must be counted some sort of success. However, late in the 1960s a new generation of directors began to emerge, amongst them Alexander Kluge and Rainer Werner Fassbinder.

Subtitled 'a film about young people's spirit of sacrifice', Hans Steinhof's *Hitlerjunge Quex* (1933) was based on the martyrdom of Hitler Youth Herbert Norkus.

The Italian Cinema

As the Second World War ended in Europe, Italy suddenly emerged from nearly a quarter of a century of government-inspired tedium in film-making to become a powerful influence in world cinema. Up to then, Italy's main contribution to the growth of the movie industry had been a spectacular series of epics made before the First World War, culminating in Giovanni Pastrone's *Cabiria* (1913).

Roberto Rossellini's *Rome, Open City* (1945), a brilliantly improvized account of Rome and her citizens under the German occupation, therefore seemed all the more of a miracle of film-making. In fact, there had already been indications that a new social criticism and concern for reality were at work in Italian films. Luchino

Visconti's *Ossessione* (1942) had met with strong disapproval from the Fascist government censors, and Vittorio de Sica, whose *Bicycle Thieves* (1948) has been considered one of the great films of all time, had also given hints of quality to come with *The Children are Watching Us* (1942–3).

Although neo-realism was largely spent as a force in Italy by the early 1950s, many of its finest achievements going unnoticed or derided by Italians who wanted escapism rather than realism in the cinema, its influence was far-reaching. Films such as Rossellini's *Paisà*, de Sica's *Shoeshine*, Alberto Lattuada's *Il Bandito*, Luigi Zampa's *Vivere in Pace* (all released in 1946), Visconti's *La Terra Trema* (1948) and de Sica's *Umberto D* (1952), written,

like most of de Sica's films, by Cesare Zavattini, are all landmarks in cinema history.

Much of the output of the Italian cinema since the great days of neo-realism has been strictly commercial: *Bread, Love . . .* and other delights with Italian beauties like Gina Lollobrigida and Sophia Loren, muscle-flexing with Steve Reeves and *Hercules*, and many fistfuls of spaghetti Westerns from the director Sergio Leone.

But the influence of the great neo-realism directors still shows in some of the work of the younger Italian directors, such as Ermanno Olmi, whose *Il Posto* (1961) brought him his first taste of international recognition, Pier Paolo Pasolini and others whose work contributes a distinctly Italian

flavour to the best world cinema. Italian directors such as Visconti, Federico Fellini and Michelangelo Antonioni are among the great directors of world cinema, whose work provides vivid commentary on the cultural mores of Western society.

The Scandinavian Cinema

All four Scandinavian countries have been involved in film-making, although only Sweden has produced films which have achieved an international market.

A star of silent films, Asta Nielsen, was Danish, but made her reputation in Germany, and Carl Dreyer, born like Nielsen in Copenhagen, directed his masterpieces in France, although he did make films in Denmark and Sweden.

Early influences on the Swedish cinema were the directors Victor Sjöström (sometimes spelt Seastrom) and Mauritz Stiller. Both made their first films in 1912 and they made about 100 between them before going to Hollywood in the 1920s. Stiller introduced Greta Garbo to the world in *The Atonement of Gösta Berling* (1924), before taking her off to America. Later Ingrid Bergman, like Garbo from Stockholm, was another Swedish gift to Hollywood.

Alf Sjöberg began the post-war boom with *Frenzy* (1944), which was written by Ingmar Bergman and starred Mai Zetterling. There was a strong sadistic theme.

Bergman became the great figure of Swedish cinema, directing his first film, *Crisis*, in 1945. The son of a parson, many of his films have strong religious themes, as in his first international success, *The Seventh Seal* (1956), a medieval morality play. *Wild Strawberries* (1957), about old age, had Victor Sjöström in the cast. Bergman's films made stars of Max Von Sydow, Gunner Björnstrand, Bibi and Harriet Andersson, Ingrid Thulin and Liv Ullman. Ullman and Bibi Andersson starred in *Persona* (1966), a haunting film about the interwoven fantasies of two women.

Recent Swedish films have taken political themes and sex as their subjects. *Elvira Madigan* (1967), directed by Bo Widerberg, and the notorious *I am Curious – Yellow* (1967), directed by Vilgot Sjöman, are two examples. Mai Zetterling, who after *Frenzy* starred in Britain, returned to Sweden to direct films sympathetic to women's liberation, the best of which is *Night Games* (1966).

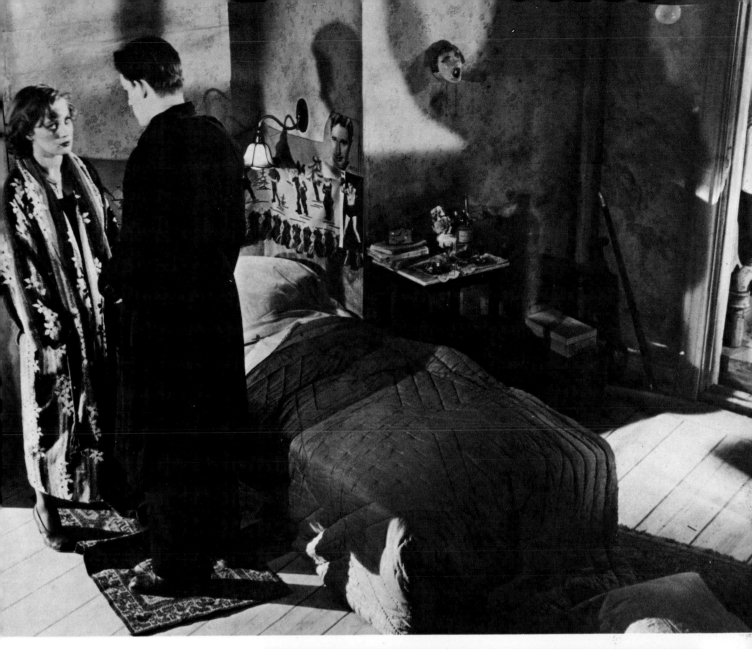

left
Jörgen Lindström becoming sexually
aroused as his mother (Ingrid Thulin)
reads to him in *Night Games* (1966).

above
Mai Zetterling in Sjöberg's *Frenzy*
(1944), Ingmar Bergman's first screenplay.

right
Early Swedish director Victor Sjöström
as an actor in Bergman's *Wild
Strawberries* (1954).

The Soviet Cinema

The Soviet Union's most creative period of film-making came in the silent era, when the art of the film was most closely allied to the needs and aspirations of the new Communist state. Among the many notable people intent on advancing both the theory and the practice of film in the 1920s, four were outstanding: Sergei Eisenstein, Vsevelod Pudovkin, Alexander Dovzhenko, and Dziga Vertov.

Eisenstein's first feature film was *Strike* (1924), which used the mass of the people as its hero. His next was *Battleship Potemkin* (1925), in which his theories of film montage and camera movement, allied to his wonderfully vigorous directing style, created a film which, fifty years later, is still considered among the best ever made.

Pudovkin made a documentary, *Mechanics of the Brain*, and *Chess Fever* in 1925 before he made *Mother* (1926), based on Maxim Gorki's novel. His *The End of St Petersburg* (1927) was made, like Eisenstein's *October* (1927), to celebrate the Tenth Anniversary of the 1917 Revolution. The

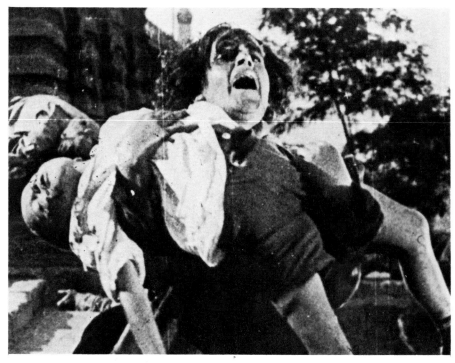

above
The 'Odessa Steps' sequence from Eisenstein's *Battleship Potemkin* (1925).

below left
Sergei Bondarchuk as Othello and Irina Skoptseva as Desdemona in Sergei Yutkevich's *Othello* (1960).

theories of constructive editing which Pudovkin put into practice in his film contrasted strongly with Eisenstein's ideas of 'intellectual montage', and formed a major area of debate within the Soviet film movement for a long time.

The Ukrainian Alexander Dovzhenko created a film style of poetic grandeur after an unlikely start with slapstick comedy, a rather silly adventure story, and *Zvenigora* (1927), a strange mixture of magic and folk-lore. He achieved his finest work with *Arsenal* (1928) and *Earth* (1930).

Vertov was the founder of the Soviet documentary tradition. His theory of the 'kino-eye'—actuality unadulterated by actors or the artifices of feature film—found its best expression in his *Man with a Movie Camera* (1928). His best work was a sound film, *Three Songs of Lenin* (1934).

In the 1930s, Soviet film-makers were to find that if the needs of the State could inspire their work, they could also stultify it. Eisenstein, Pudovkin, Dovzhenko and Vertov all encountered State disapproval of their theories and methods. Eisenstein completed nothing between *The Old and the New* (1929) and *Alexander Nevsky* (1938) apart from the results of his disastrous collaboration with Upton Sinclair in Mexico, *Que Viva Mexico!* The undue influence of the State on their work has been a problem for Soviet film-makers ever since.

During a relatively short-lived period in the 1950s and 1960s, when the State relaxed its grip on the ideological content of films, several fine films were made. Russians were given a realistic view of the Second World War in films such as Mikhail Kalatozov's *The Cranes are Flying* (1957) and Grigori Chukrai's *Ballad of a Soldier* (1959). Other films made at this time, and which achieved international success, included Yosif Heifitz's *The Lady with the Little Dog* (1960) and Grigori Kozintsev's *Don Quixote* (1957) and *Hamlet* (1964), one of the cinema's finest accounts of a Shakespeare play.

top
'Alas! poor Yorick.' Innokenty Smoktunovsky as Hamlet and V. Kolpakor as the grave-digger in Grigori Kozintsev's superb *Hamlet* (1964).

left
Alexander Dovzhenko's *Earth* (1930).

The Eastern European Cinema

The Second World War was a watershed in East European cinema. Before it only Czechoslovakia and Hungary had film industries of any size, the former known mostly for Gustav Machatý's controversial *Extase* (1933), its staple diet of farce and operetta, its radical cartoons and its documentaries, and the latter for the sentimental formula comedies of the 1930s and its fundamentally 'literary' approach to the cinema. After the war, and the establishment of the socialist states, the film industries of Czechoslovakia, Hungary, Poland, Yugoslavia, and Romania were taken into state control and so began the experience which produced some of the most stimulating world cinema of the 1960s.

To Yugoslavia and Romania, nationalization brought vital opportunities for training in film techniques and for cinema building. By the 1950s, Yugoslavian animators working in Zagreb had become world famous, and a thriving group of documentary-makers was based on Belgrade. Animation has also brought Romania its greatest successes to date.

For Czechoslovakia, Poland, and to a lesser extent Hungary, all with a pre-war tradition of film-making, state control very soon meant a new vulnerability to political pressure. Throughout the Eastern bloc strict instruction was given concerning the role of cinema in a socialist state, and a barren form of social realism, show-

ing man in his daily life and demonstrating the virtues of socialism, prevailed. However, after the death of Stalin in 1953 and the Twentieth Party Congress in 1956, official attitudes relaxed somewhat, and the change was apparent in a more philosophical approach to historical subjects and in a freedom to deal with contemporary themes without socialist stereotypes.

Hungary reached a high point in 1955–6, with important directors such as Zoltan Fabri and Felix Mariassy. There was a lull after the Russian invasion of 1956, but by 1963 a new generation of directors was emerging, due in large part to official encouragement. Miklós Jancsó and András

left
Zbigniew Cybulski in *Ashes and Diamonds* (1958). Director Andrzej Wajda examines the problems of peace on the day Poland is liberated.

above
Red Psalm (1971), directed by Hungary's Miklós Jancsó. The inevitable triumph of just revolution is the theme of this account of a peasant uprising.

Kovács have remained significant in a group characterized by its liking for socio-political debate. Czechoslovakia's 'new wave' directors of the early 1960s, amongst whom Miloš Forman and Jiří Menzel made the biggest international names, were more concerned to present intimate studies of contemporary life. Cinema here has not yet recovered from the events of 1968. The early 1960s were, by contrast, a crisis period for the Polish film industry. De-Stalinization had thrown up Andrzej Munk and Andrzej Wajda, but by 1963 Roman Polański was judging it politic to continue his career in the West. Nevertheless, Polish cinema has achieved a recognizably 'national' quality – a romantic undercurrent of violence and symbolism. By the 1960s, Yugoslavia was increasing her feature output and the work of Dušan Makavejev demonstrates the concern with social structures and individual versus collective responsibility which underpins the new East European cinema.

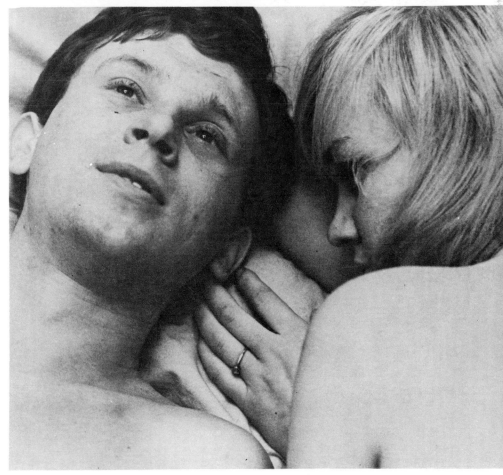

Miloš Forman's *A Blonde in Love* (1965), with Vladimir Pucholt and Jana Brejchová. An ironic but sympathetic look at romantic illusion and contemporary Czech society.

The Indian and Japanese Cinema

The Indian film industry is really a collection of separate industries, as the cultural and language differences between the various regions do not allow a national film identity. Social conventions and severe censorship have restricted development and experimental films, and the output is largely for the home market – a not inconsiderable one. Over 300 films are produced annually, mainly from Bombay, Madras and Calcutta, despite heavy government tax. Films reached India through agents of the Lumières in 1896, and the first Indian feature film, *Raja Harischandra*, was made by Dhundiraj Govind Phalke in 1912. The first film to be acclaimed internationally was *Pather Panchali* (1954), directed by Satyajit Ray, the first of a trilogy. The second part, *The Unvanquished* (1956), won the Grand Prix at the Venice Film Festival. Their success led to the Film Finance Corporation, which makes money available to producers, thus ensuring the domestic industry flourishes. Ray remains the only international figure.

The highly commercial Japanese industry, with an output matching India's, has produced many international figures. The first Japanese film to have a great success in the West

above right
Satyajit Ray's 1954 film *Pather Panchali* (Song of the Road) was about life in a Bengal village seen through the eyes of a young boy and girl.

right
Machiko Kyo as the phantom princess and Masayuki Mori as the bewitched potter in Mizoguchi's *Ugetsu Monogatari* (1953).

opposite
Toshiro Mifune (*left*) encounters Ko Kimura (*centre*) and Takashi Shimura, and claims he is a fellow samurai in Kurosawa's *The Seven Samurai* (1954).

was *Rashomon* (1950), directed by Akira Kurosawa, about the ways people react to violence. Kurosawa had an even greater success with the classic *The Seven Samurai* (1954), an Academy Award-winning three-hour account of samurai hired to defend a village. Toshiro Mifune and Takashi Shimura became actors with Western identities. The acclaim accorded *Rashomon* at the Venice Film Festival led to recognition of other Japanese masterpieces. Kenji Mizoguchi was at his peak when he died in 1956, just two years after he had won a Venice award with *Ugetsu Monogatari* (1953), a ghost story. Kon Ichikawa won an award at Venice with *The Burmese Harp* (1955), an anti-war film about a soldier who turns priest. He also directed the story of the *Tokyo Olympiad* (1965). Yasujiro Ozu ranks with Mizoguchi and Kurosawa among Japan's greatest directors, and his best-known film is *Tokyo Story* (1953). The new wave of Japanese directors fighting the threats of television and the market demand for pornography is led by Nagisa Oshima, whose successes include *The Ceremony* (1970).

Central and South American Cinema

Before 1959 cinema in Central and South America had mainly local interest. Names that did make the world scene include Spanish director Luis Buñuel, who first went to Mexico in 1947 and made some of his major films there (*Los Olvidados*, 1950; *Nazarin*, 1959; *El Angel Exterminador*, 1962); Alberto Cavalcanti, director and set designer, who returned to his native Brazil in 1949 in an attempt to rally the film industry but had his greatest successes elsewhere (in France in the 1920s and in Britain in the 1930s and 1940s); and Argentinian-born Leopoldo Torre Nilsson, who by the 1960s had already revealed a baroque line in social criticism with films like *La Casa del Angel* (1957). But for the most part Latin American cinema had for years concentrated on cheaply-made, highly commercial entertainment. Brazil had the kind of schmaltzy 'folk-lore' tradition typified by Carmen Miranda; Mexico's scenic beauty was the ideal setting for umpteen location dramatics; and cosmopolitan Cuba turned out technically accomplished blue movies.

In March 1959 the organization of every aspect of Cuban cinema was given to the Instituto Cubano del Arte e Industria Cinematographicos. This, the first ideological/cultural act of the new revolutionary government, was clear recognition of the political power of film. Not a new approach of course, the Russians had done the same over forty years before – but it may well have been the catalyst South America needed. Certainly the most interesting new films coming out of Brazil, Bolivia and Argentina have in common the belief that film-making is a political act. Outstanding examples

Leopoldo Torre Nilsson's *The Hand in the Trap* (1961), a study of corrupt aristocracy. A brilliant stylist, Nilsson has won more recognition abroad than in his native Argentina.

left
Bureaucracy seen through the satirical eye of Cuban director Tomás Gutiérrez Alea. *The Death of a Bureaucrat* (1966) is farce, and full of references to film history.

include Solanas and Getino's *La Hora de los Hornos* (Argentina, 1968) and Jorge Sanjines' *Blood of the Condor* (Bolivia, 1971). Both were produced and distributed outside the normal commercial channels; both assume political awareness triggers political action and set about erecting 'the springboard for liberation'. Brazil has possibly the strongest new cinema movement in South America, led by Glauber Rocha, film critic and direc-

tor, and its aim, pursued in the face of stiff censorship, is to represent the political and social realities of Brazilian life today.

Much of Cuba's own output has been educational or propagandizing, and cinema has gone mobile in an attempt to reach the rural illiterate. Tomás Gutiérrez Alea, Humberto Solas, and Manuel Octavio Gomez are among the most talented directors to have emerged since the revolution.

Antonio das Mortes (1968), directed by Brazil's Glauber Rocha. The hero, an assassin hired by a tyrannical landlord to kill his rebellious peasantry, decides to join them instead.

167

Ten Great Directors

David Wark Griffith (1875–1948)

The Birth of a Nation (1915) and *Intolerance* (1916) are Griffith's finest films, but it is his earlier work in hundreds of unmemorable comedies, melodramas, Westerns, thrillers, and romances which earns him the title of great director. Any description of his achievement tends to degenerate into a catalogue of 'firsts'. The close-up, the long shot, the fade out, the use of masks to frame images, cutting between parallel action – Griffith cannot claim to have invented them all but he did discover their potential when he used them to shape cinema narrative. Before D. W. a movie was simply a filmed play; a camera was set up in place of an audience and scene followed scene just as they did in the theatre. Afterwards there was a language which could be used to emphasize action or emotion, reveal character, evoke atmosphere. The cinema had come of age.

Babylon, Hollywood-style, the set for one of Griffith's four sequences illustrating the timeless working of *Intolerance* (1916).

168

Fritz Lang
(1890–   )

Many people dismiss Lang's Hollywood career as a sell-out to commercialism. German silents like *The Nibelungen Saga* (1924) and *Metropolis* (1926) are praised for their beauty and imagination, whereas the mixture of Westerns, thrillers, and psychological mysteries that makes up the bulk of his American films is quietly deplored, if it is discussed at all. But this is to miss two central facts about Lang. He has always aimed his work at a wide general audience (most of his German films were financial as well as critical successes), and however apparently unpromising his

material he always used it as the basis for an examination of certain recurring themes. The individual alone in a hostile environment, the individual divided within, situations in which innocence becomes guilt and justice injustice – these preoccupations crop up again and again throughout Lang's career.

opposite
Child-murderer Peter Lorre meets his accusers in Fritz Lang's *M* (1931).

John Ford (1895–1973)

'He made Westerns' – that was the epitaph Ford himself suggested, and a great many people would go along with it. *Stagecoach* (1939) appears in everybody's list of top ten Westerns, while the series made between 1946 and 1951 is regularly celebrated in words like 'classic' and 'poetic'. But what about the long period in the 1930s when he didn't make a single Western? And the four Best Director Oscars – for *The Informer* (1935), *The Grapes of Wrath* (1940), *How Green Was My Valley* (1941), and *The Quiet Man* (1952), not one of them with a stagecoach in sight? Clearly as a

definition it won't do. Ford is great because throughout a long career spent in Hollywood, the so-called boneyard of all talent, he explored an entirely personal philosophy. Morality was his concern, the bedrock morality that separates civilization from savagery, order from chaos. And with a severe economy of narrative and characterization and a precise, symbolic use of setting, he examined the moments when men and women are forced to work their own survival.

above
Ford's *She Wore a Yellow Ribbon* (1949). John Wayne sees out his last days as a cavalry officer in a changing world. Joanne Dru was the girl of the title.

Sergei Mikhailovitch Eisenstein (1898–1948)

Eisenstein's reputation as a great Russian director rests upon three silent films: *Strike* (1924), *Battleship Potemkin* (1925), and *October* (1927). It is the force and energy of his editing technique in passages like the massacre on the Odessa Steps in *Potemkin* and the flight over the drawbridge in *October* which impress. Griffith had wanted to tell a story in cinematic terms and had varied and arranged his shots to do this as effectively as possible. Eisenstein, in common with other Soviet directors, was intent on teaching and inspiring his audience by forcing it 'to think in a certain direction'. He believed that a scene's dynamics derived from a sequence of intellectual shocks or surprises, and his aim when editing material was to set shots in opposition to one another so as to create a 'spark' or new thought. His three great early films demonstrate an increasing use of this theory of montage.

above
Eisenstein's *October* (1927).

right
Nikolai Cherkassov in Eisenstein's *Ivan the Terrible* (1944–6).

In Hawks' comedies it's the men who come off worst. Katharine Hepburn was the source of most of the mayhem in *Bringing Up Baby* (1938). Scientist Cary Grant keeps an eye open for her dog – it's buried his prehistoric bone.

Howard Hawks (1896–)

Hawks began directing movies almost fifty years ago and he's made no great innovations or shown no signs of tremendous personal development yet. What he has done, quite simply, is to make some of the most entertaining films ever to come out of Hollywood. Action dramas like *To Have and Have Not* (1944) and *The Big Sleep* (1946) and pacey comedies such as *Bringing Up Baby* (1938) and *His Girl Friday*

(1940) have gone down particularly well, but he has worked in most of the established genres. Hawks resists all attempts to be solemn about his work, insisting that film-making is just 'fun', but it is possible to trace certain constant preoccupations in the self-sufficient all-male groups of the action movies and the sex and role reversals of the comedies. His films, in fact, have a peculiarly masculine tone and suggest a belief in each man's need for the self-respect that comes from self-determination.

right
Renoir's *Toni* (1934) anticipates Italian neo-realism in its use of non-professional actors and real settings.

below
Carette (*left*) in *La Règle du Jeu* (1939), Renoir's great comedy of manners.

Jean Renoir (1894–   )

It is generally for his work in the 1930s – from *La Chienne* (1931) to *La Règle du Jeu* (1939) – that Renoir earns the title Greatest French Director. Whether in the anarchic comedy of *Bondu Sauvé des Eaux* (1932) or the French Communist Party manifesto *La Vie est à Nous* (1936) his social concern marks him out a serious director. The expression of that concern makes him great. Rejecting the

Griffith/Eisenstein tradition of montage, he found a more casual, naturalistic style which allowed the actor to dictate camera movement. The performance was, he believed, the core of the film, and he encouraged improvization. Technique was the big enemy because it destroyed vitality, and the films evolved out of Renoir's communication with his actors. It's an approach which encapsulates the humanity of the man who once said, 'The only thing I can bring to this illogical, irresponsible and cruel universe is my love.'

Ingrid Bergman and Jean Marais in *Eléna et les Hommes* (1956), a less bitter but still satirical look at the rich and ambitious.

Alfred Hitchcock (1899–   )

'Master of suspense' is the tag most often applied to Hitchcock, and minutely detailed pre-production planning has kept his audiences on the edge of their seats for almost fifty years. But for Hitchcock suspense is a tool, not an end in itself. Suspense means audience involvement and Hitchcock needs that because what he wants us to know is how it feels to be guilty, insecure, and fearful. His greatest films – *Rear Window* (1954), *Vertigo* (1958), and *Psycho* (1960) – all brilliantly exploit our identification with flawed protagonists in such a way that we emerge disturbed by the ambiguity of our responses. Careful narrative detail and a subjective camera are the basis of the technique. A predominant theme in much of his work is the notion that danger lurks close beneath the ordinary surface of

James Stewart descends the tower in Hitchcock's *Vertigo* (1958), with a dizzying camera angle to underline the character's phobia.

life. From it springs his penchant for casting 'good guys' like James Stewart and Cary Grant in morally suspect roles and it is also the source of an exciting non-cliché like the crop-sprayer pursuit of Grant in *North by Northwest* (1959).

above
Tim Holt and Dolores Costello, mother and son in *The Magnificent Ambersons* (1942), a lament, said Welles, 'not so much for the epoch as for the sense of moral values which are destroyed.'

right
Orson Welles as *Citizen Kane* (1940).

Orson Welles (1915–   )

Citizen Kane (1940) was Welles' first Hollywood film; it's also probably his greatest, though comparisons may be unjust because he has never again had the freedom or the resources he had then. Most of the other Hollywood pictures were ruthlessly cut, and his European productions always seem to teeter on the brink of insolvency. The techniques used in *Kane* were not new; deep-focus lenses allowing simultaneous action on different planes of vision, forceful camera movement, distorted images, a story told in flashback, they had all been used before. What makes *Citizen Kane* such a startling achievement is its pace and its intensity, an intensity that originates in a consistently organized personal style. The fireworks may never have been quite as bright again, but the theme of self-deception is deepened and defined in ever-widening circles through all his subsequent work.

Michelangelo Antonioni (1912–)

Antonioni's impact on European cinema in the 1960s was considerable. International recognition came with *L'Avventura* (1959), but his earlier work reveals a steady progress in terms of content and style towards what is undoubtedly his most successful film to date. His theme is the threat which the modern world poses to fundamental human sentiments, his milieu (for the most part) the monied and intellectual middle classes, and his concern the description of emotional and mental states through behaviour. With an exceedingly plain camera technique and a reliance on real time, Antonioni follows his characters 'beyond the moments conventionally considered important to show them even when everything appears to have been said.' *La Notte* (1961), *L'Eclisse* (1962), and *Il Deserto Rosso* (1964) sustain the same highly individual approach. Much of Antonioni's mature work has an underlying tranced, dream-like quality. In his latest films, *Il Deserto Rosso*, *Blow-Up* (1966), and *Zabriskie Point* (1969), he seems to be deliberately heightening it to express the disconnection at the heart of contemporary society.

above
Zabriskie Point (1969), Antonioni's look at student revolt in America. The guy is Mark Frechette.

left
Monica Vitti and Gabriele Ferzetti in Antonioni's *L'Avventura* (1959). She can't forget his girl (her friend) disappeared only three days ago.

opposite top
Crisis in the Pentagon War Room. Russian ambassador (Peter Bull), General Turgidson (George C. Scott), and the U.S. President (Peter Sellers) discuss tactics in Kubrick's *Dr Strangelove* (1963).

opposite bottom
James Mason doing what comes naturally in *Lolita* (Kubrick, 1962).

Stanley Kubrick
(1928–   )

Kubrick is the most exciting new talent to have come out of America in years. His ability to express ideas in forms which reflect his meaning is apparent in the black comedy of *Dr Strangelove* (1963), where grotesque and surreal figures act out their own obsessions, blind to the threat of nuclear war. His camerawork, often praised for its technical brilliance, reveals the same submergence of form in meaning, as, for instance, in the use of subtly distorting wide-angle lenses through parts of *A Clockwork Orange* (1971). Predictably, he enjoys editing more than any other film-making process, but he insists on planning control of an entire project from conception to première, his one experience of holding someone else's baby, *Spartacus* (1960), only confirming his fears. His most original film to date is *2001: A Space Odyssey* (1968). A 'mythical documentary' about the concept of intelligence, it is a strikingly visual movie (forty minutes of dialogue and a three-hour running time) which must be felt rather than analysed.

Avant-garde and Underground Films

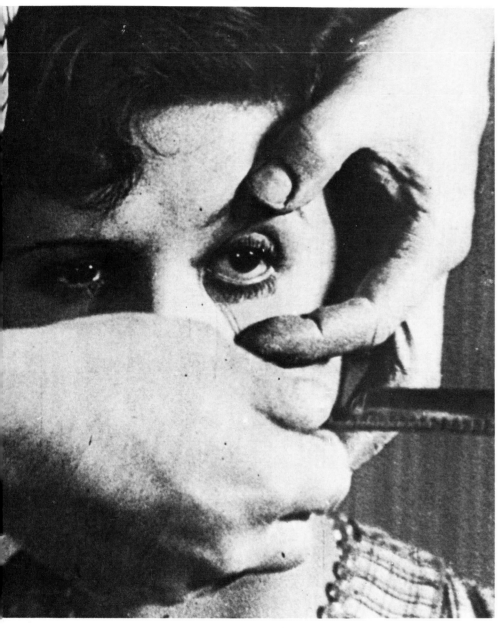

Society is blinded by convention — only through violence shall we see: a surreal image from Buñuel's *Un Chien Andalou* (1928).

Definitions of 'avant-garde' and 'underground' cinema don't come easily. Certainly, it's true to say both are personal cinema, peripheral to the mainstream development of the film, and that 'avant-garde' is used mainly to describe various French movements of the 1920s and early 1930s, whereas the term 'underground' relates to an international phenomenon which had its beginnings in the United States in the late 1950s. But that's hardly enough. Avant-garde cinema had a high regard for film craftsmanship and addressed itself to a cultural élite fully aware of current artistic forms and conventions. Much underground cinema rejects polished technique, as it rejects Hollywood gloss, and, although not greatly concerned with accessibility, speaks to a much wider, younger audience disenchanted with pre-packaged television entertainment. The avant-garde remained a small, relatively localized, informal movement. Underground cinema has gone international, organized itself into co-operatives, and (in the United States at least) is now more healthy than the commercial industry. However, avant-garde and underground cinema do have one thing in common and it is important. Both value freedom of expression and, since both frequently operate in the taboo areas of human communication (in particular in sex), both challenge censorship.

There were two separate avant-garde movements in France in the 1920s and early 1930s, and the first, the Impressionist movement, came to an end in 1924 with the death of its leading theorist, Louis Delluc. He had argued that film was essentially a visual medium, and that to think of it merely as words plus pictures was to waste its incomparable ability to create illusion. Marcel l'Herbier was his truest disciple, in early films like *L'Homme du Large* (1920), but Abel Gance, Germaine Dulac, and Jean Epstein also show signs of his influence. The second, and stronger, movement originated in the peculiarly rich environment of artistic experiment that was France in the 1920s.

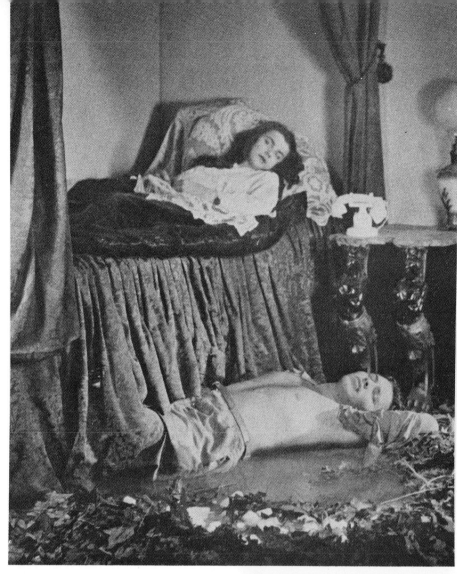

left
Dreams that Money Can Buy (1944–7) was a late survival of the avant-garde. Made in the U.S. by German emigré Hans Richter, it was a series of separate episodes directed by Fernand Léger, Marcel Duchamp, Max Ernst, Man Ray, and Alexander Calder.

right
Lelia Goldoni and Anthony Ray in John Cassavetes' *Shadows* (1960). A film from the New York documentary stable, it mixed professionals and amateurs and relied heavily on improvization.

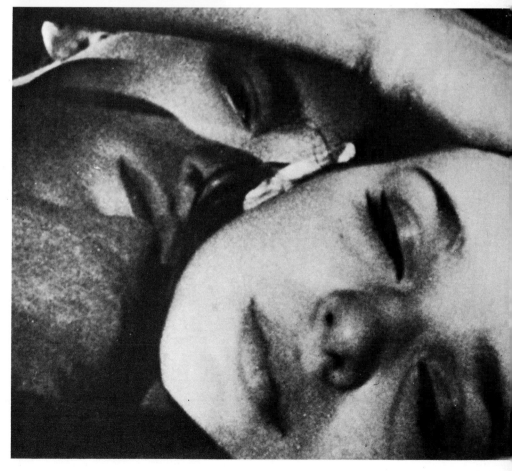

Dadaism and, later, Surrealism had the profoundest effects. René Clair in *Entr'acte* (1924), shooting his ballerina from below to reveal her panties and showing her for an instant bearded, was practising true Dadaism in his intention to create shock, surprise, and laughter. Other exponents included Man Ray, and Fernand Léger and Dudley Murphy. Surrealism's chief, most savage adherent was Luis Buñuel. *Un Chien Andalou* (1928, Salvador Dali co-wrote) and *L'Age d'Or* (1930) both use the free association of the unconscious mind to create a series of powerful cinematic images. Jean Vigo, Germaine Dulac, Fernand Léger, and Marcel Duchamp also

right
Andy Warhol's *Women in Revolt* (1971),
a discussion of women's liberation with
transvestites playing the women's roles.

below
James Broughton's *The Bed* (1967), a
happy tribute to human sexuality.

worked in this field. Gradually, the movement declined, as experimentalists went commercial or moved into animation and documentary. Apart from France, only Germany had any significant avant-garde at this time – Hans Richter, Viking Eggeling, Walter Ruttmann, and Oskar Fischinger were all interested in abstract film-making, a link with the underground movement of today.

That movement evolved mainly from the groups of experimentalists working in New York and on the West Coast of the United States in the 1940s. Maya Deren was a leading figure and other important names included James Broughton, Chris Harrington, Hans Richter, Marie Menken, Willard Maas, and Gregory Markopoulos. However, the New York documentary school of the 1950s and early 1960s, working outside the normal commercial channels to produce studies of deprivation in American society, was also influential.

It is not easy to generalize about themes or treatment in the underground movement. Homosexuality in Jack Smith's *Flaming Creatures* (1963), Gregory Markopoulos' *The Iliac Passion* (1967), and Andy Warhol's *Lonesome Cowboys* (1969); sexual deviation in Kenneth Anger's *Scorpio Rising* (1963); the visual and sensual effects of repeated superimposition in Ron Rice's *Senseless* (1962) and Stan Brakhage's *Dog Star Man* (1959–64); real-time studies of objective reality in Warhol's *Sleep* (1963) and Brakhage's 'portrait' pictures; montages of old film-stock in Bruce Connor's *Cosmic*

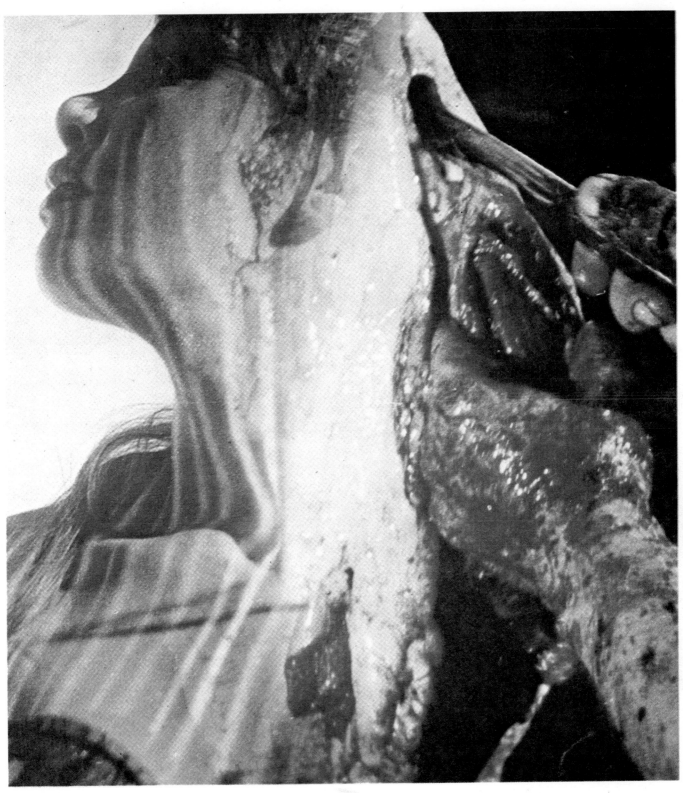

Ray (1961), Robert Nelson's *Oh Dem Watermelons* (1965), and Ben Van Meter's *Up Tight... L.A. is Burning... Shit* (1966); experiments on the physiological effects of variations in light in Tony Conrad's *The Flicker* (1965) and colour in Paul Sharits' *Ray Gun Virus* (1966); and the expanded cinema of Stan Vanderbeek with its multi-projection and mixed-media presentation – these are just a few of the more notable parallels within the movement.

The American underground sur-faced around 1966, due to the wider distribution networks established by Jonas Mekas and Bruce Baillie and the increasingly 'commercial' ap-proach of the Warhol combine. The late 1960s saw underground film-making established in Italy, Germany, and France (and to a lesser degree in Britain, Japan, Holland, Austria, Canada, and Switzerland) but as yet no other country rivals the scale and organization of the American under-ground.

Herostratus (1967). Directed by Don Levy, an Australian living in Great Britain, the film attacks the circle of self-destruction inherent in a society based on selfish, personal ends.

Censorship and the Cinema

In the main, film censorship originates from three sources: government, organized religion, and the film industry itself.

Government censorship can be national, as in India, where since 1949 a central board has been in operation, or regional, as in France, where local authorities have the right to ban within their own districts. It may be applied for ideological reasons; in Soviet Russia, for instance, cinema was for years regarded as 'the keenest weapon ... of the socialist transformation of the world and man.' It may also be used for overtly political reasons, such as the Brazilian reaction to the socially critical work of its *cinema nôvo* directors, the initial banning in many European countries of Soviet classics like *Battleship Potemkin* (1925) and *Mother* (1926), and the suppression of films dealing with black-white sexual relationships in South Africa. Or for

left
Czech Gustav Machatý's *Extase* (*Ecstasy*, 1933) hit state censorship problems when it reached America in 1934. It wasn't Hedwig Kiesler's nudity that caused the trouble so much as close-ups of her face during sexual intercourse.

top right
The Outlaw (1943) was the first movie to challenge the Hollywood production code by coming out without a seal of approval. The fact that it still made money encouraged others to follow suit.

right
Mae West's Hollywood career was dogged by censorship battles in the 1930s. She wrote her own dialogue, and lines like 'Is that a gun in your pocket or are you just pleased to see me?' didn't endear her to the industry's Hays Office. Here she is with Ivan Lebedeff and Marjorie Gateson in *Goin' to Town* (1935).

TALL.... TERRIFIC.... and TROUBLE!

OWARD HUGHES' Daring PRODUCTION

The Outlaw

INTRODUCING
JANE RUSSELL

JACK BUETEL
THOMAS MITCHELL
WALTER HUSTON

UNITED ARTISTS

right
Song of Russia (1943), a victim of
political censorship in the U.S. Although
just an averagely mindless love story
about an American orchestral conductor
on tour in Russia, the film was labelled
'pernicious' by the House of
Representatives Un-American Activities
Committee in 1947.

below right
The beggars' Last Supper from Luis
Buñuel's *Viridiana* (1961): the climax of
a film the Spanish government banned
because of its sacrilege and violent
anticlericalism.

ethical considerations, such as the
Indian Congress Party's desire to see
cinema play its part in 'the building
up of a healthy national life'.

Organized religion, when it enters
the field of censorship, is generally
concerned with two challenges to its
authority: the 'technical' sins of sacrilege, blasphemy, etc., and sins against
its code of moral conduct. The Catholic Church, for instance, has played a
dominant role in Ireland, in Spain,
and in the United States, where since
1933 the Legion of Decency (re-
named the National Catholic Office
for Motion Pictures in the 1960s) has
fretted the industry.

Self-protection from governmental
or religious interference has been the
primary reason for self-regulation.
Boards such as the British Board of
Film Censors (founded in 1912) and
the Motion Picture Producers and
Distributors' Association of America
(founded in 1921 and often known as
the Hays Office after Will Hays, its
first President) were created to protect

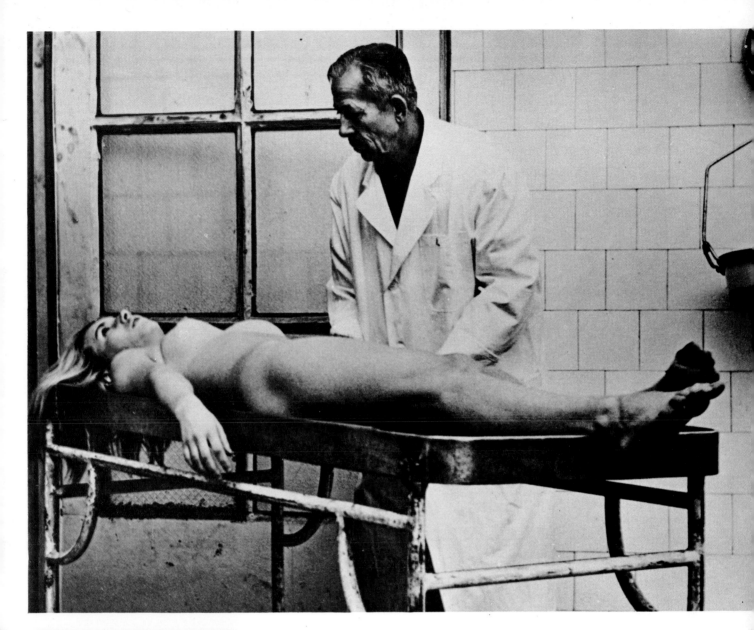

heavy investment, and have often demonstrated a greater concern with marketability than with what might be called artistic integrity.

The machinery of censorship differs widely and is obviously subject to alteration. A film may be controlled through various stages of its production, or it may simply be examined before exhibition. The Russian scriptwriter Smirnova complained that under the harsh restraints of Stalinist social realism a script had to be inspected by twenty-eight officials before it went to the studio art council; the Nazi Reich Film Law of 1934 ordered the scrutiny of scripts before production; and America and Britain kept a tight control on the new films coming out of West Germany and Japan after the Second World War.

In Britain a dual system of censorship operates. The industry's watchdog, the BBFC, examines all films intended for public exhibition and classifies them, either with or without

In the mid-1960s the BBFC began pursuing a policy of non-interference in the 'quality' market but they soon came a cropper over Eva Ras's pubic hair in *The Switchboard Operator* (1967). Underestimating Yugoslav Dušan Makavejev's work, they cut savagely and earned critical derision. The effect was an immediate relaxation in the Board's attitude to female nudity.

modification, or bans them. Government, in the form of de-centralized local authorities, has power to reverse the board's decisions. It sounds topsy-turvy, but its defenders claim it has the great advantage of flexibility. In the United States the situation is even more complicated. Not only is there a strong Catholic lobby and an industry-based examining board, but since 1915 and the judgement in the Mutual v Ohio case there has been a series of conflicting decisions which give varying degrees of status to state and city censorship boards. Some countries, amongst them the United States, France, India, West Germany and Britain, have, at certain times, had a written code which itemized taboo subjects and/or treatments; others operate more informally.

During the past fifteen years there has been a slackening of censorship controls (particularly in sexual matters) in many countries. Indeed there is no longer any censorship at all in Belgium, Denmark, Sweden, West Germany, and certain parts of Switzerland. One recent and popular method of lifting censorship is to restrict the audience, rather than the film. This can be done by forbidding people under a certain age to view a film (except, sometimes, under stipulated conditions) or by only permitting unlicensed screenings in private clubs. (There is, of course, often an age limitation on club membership, but club showings have the additional advantage that their audiences are specialized and, therefore, less likely to be shocked.)

Britain first introduced an age restriction in 1951 – the X-certificate film was not open to children under the age of sixteen. The grading system adopted then was subsequently altered to that in operation today (U, A, AA, and X films). Film industries have never been eager to do anything which might restrict their audiences, so it is not surprising that similar action was a long time coming in the United States. However, when the SMA (Suggested for Mature Audiences) tag disappeared fast beneath a flood of 'adult' subject matter in the three years following its introduction in 1965, a system of film classification seemed the only answer and Jack Valenti (president of the by now MPAA) brought in his G, GP, R, and X codings.

above
Stanley Kubrick's *A Clockwork Orange* (1971) was a controversial film in the British debate on violence in the movies. Many people felt it should have been cut much further.

top right
Marlon Brando and Maria Schneider in Bernardo Bertolucci's *Last Tango in Paris* (1972). Spaniards bussed over the border into France when the film was banned in Spain.

right
It was the language that caused the problems in Joseph Strick's film version of James Joyce's *Ulysses* (1967). Ireland banned the film; the BBFC made cuts; and New Zealand licensed it for segregated (male and female) audiences. Seen here are Barbara Jefford (Molly Bloom) and Maurice Roeves.

Images of Stardom

Movie stars are part of the mythology of the twentieth century. Gods and goddesses from an exotic world ordinary mortals can only imagine, they have imparted their charisma, their indefinable magic to areas of experience far beyond the confines of the cinema.

Miss Florence Lawrence was the first real movie star. She became so because she was not killed by a streetcar in St Louis in 1910. If she was the victim of anything, it was of the publicity machinations of Carl Laemmle, the boss of her new studio, Imp. He had lured her from Biograph, where she had been billed as the 'Biograph Girl', and to make sure that the world knew that she was now part of the Imp set-up he arranged that the story of her 'death' should be published simply so that he could refute it as sensationally as possible. The scheme worked, and Miss Lawrence was a star – for a time.

The early companies – Edison, Biograph, Vitagraph, and the other companies which made up the Motion Picture Patent Company – had wanted their actors to remain anonymous, largely to keep them dependent on the company and therefore inexpensive. But the public wanted otherwise. They wished to know the names of the men and women they saw on the screen, and the smaller, independent film companies obliged them by naming their stars.

So quickly did the star system take hold that by the time the First World War ended, it was the most important factor in the movies. Stars like Mary Pickford and Charlie Chaplin were often the sole reason for the sale of their pictures to exhibitors and cinemas in America and Europe, and thus they could command huge salaries from the companies to whom they were contracted.

The 1920s was the time of the great stars – Pickford, Fairbanks, Chaplin, the Gish sisters, Valentino, Garbo were world figures. The fan magazines, which began life as the house magazines of the film companies, contributed to the star legend, while the box-office receipts and the fan mail which poured into the studios told the bosses who the top stars were,

who was fading, and whose new face they should take more notice of. By the 1930s, the star system, as much as the stars themselves, was the foundation of the industry. Studio bosses had countered stars' demands for high salaries with contracts running several years and no escape clauses. Bette Davis' lost law suit in 1936 against Warner Brothers, whose contract with her obliged her to work only for them until 1942 (she wanted to make a picture in Britain), was a *cause célèbre* at the time.

The star system lasted into the 1950s and 1960s, but now it has gone. Movie actors have become impressarios

and directors. The studios which once bound them with long-term contracts are no longer the autocrats they were and the contracts have changed. The growth of internationalism in film-making, the death of the B-feature, the growth of television, have all helped cause the death of the system.

The stars remain, of course. Names like Steve McQueen and Robert Redford, Liza Minnelli and Barbra Streisand, will always help sell a movie to the public. But they are not gods and goddesses any more. They have come down to our level.

Lillian Gish (1896–   ) made her stage debut at the age of five, and in 1912 appeared in her first film, *The Unseen Enemy*. Most of her early films were made with D. W. Griffith, and she was in *The Birth of a Nation* (1915). Other successes were *Broken Blossoms* (1919), *The Big Parade* (1926) and *The Scarlet Letter* (1926). She had a delicate, spiritual beauty and great acting ability, and was at her best as

frail but passionate heroines bravely facing terror and tragedy. Although she tried to adapt to the talkies, her style of acting became out of date, and her starring roles were in the silents. Nevertheless, she was still making films in the 1960s. Her sister, Dorothy, also had a successful screen career, and the two made films together. The still is from Victor Sjöström's *The Wind* (1928).

Jane Fonda (1937–   ) is very much a modern star. Her views on sex, women's liberation and politics are cogent and firmly expressed, and publicized in a way which might have destroyed the career of an old-style love goddess, but which in these days gain her admirers. Some of her films have been poor, others very good. Among the best are *Cat Ballou* (1965), *Barefoot in the Park* (1967), in which she showed a fine style in comedy, *They Shoot Horses, Don't They?* (1969) and *Klute* (1971) in which she played a call-girl, as illustrated here, and for which she won an Oscar. She is a daughter of Henry Fonda, and sister of Peter Fonda.

James Dean (1931–1955) starred in only three films, made in two years. The day after completing the third he was killed in a car smash. At the time of his violent death a cult of youth was gaining momentum. In two of his films he had played a youth in rebellion, with much force and passion. These circumstances combined to cause a wave of idolatry after his death, and he became a symbol of a generation. It is still difficult to decide how good he was, or how good he might have become. His films were *East of Eden* (1955), *Rebel Without a Cause* (1955) and *Giant* (1956).

Douglas Fairbanks (1883–1939), whose son also had a successful career, made his screen debut in 1915. He was popular from the start with his exuberance, charm and athleticism, but it was *The Mark of Zorro* (1920), in which he played a dashing swordsman, that established his supreme reputation as a swashbuckler. Similar films followed, the best being *Robin Hood* (1922) and *The Thief of Bagdad* (1924). He established United Artists with Chaplin, Griffith and Mary Pickford, whom he married. They were folk-heroes, the most famous and popular married couple in films. His films began to decline in the late 1920s. In the photograph he is D'Artagnan in *The Three Musketeers* (1921), for which he grew (and kept) his moustache.

The fan magazines were instrumental in establishing the stars, particularly in the 1920s and 1930s. Film-goers were greedy for any details of their lives, and studios were anxious to obtain as much publicity as possible for the stars who were their assets. The studios and magazines co-operated in publishing scandals, false or real, denials, equally true or false, gossip, publicity material and other inventions, often only half-believed by the readers, but nonetheless eagerly sought. Film stars were natural cover-girls (or men). Some of the delights contained inside can be read on these early covers: 'The Studio Secrets', 'Valentino's Hollywood Life' and 'Whose Heart is Whose in Hollywood'. The article 'How to Hold Your Youth' was not advertising an early version of *The Graduate*.

MOTION PICTURE
CLASSIC

25

PICTURE PLAY

NOV. 1927

LITTLE JOURNEYS TO FILMLAND

The Truth About Salar

GRETA

CINEMA

THE MAGAZINE OF THE PHOTOPLAY

Motion Picture

25 CENTS

The Talkies
First Birthd

hoopee
Book

The National Guide to Motion Pictures

PHOTOPLAY

October 1928

A BREWSTER PUBLICATION

MOTION PICTURE

MAGAZINE

THE
QUALITY MAGAZINE
OF THE SCREEN

DECEMBER
25

Ramon Novarro

ION PICTURE

MAGAZINE
I Shilling

QUALITY MAGAZINE OF THE SCREEN

ONS of an INTERVIEWER

The World's Leading Moving Picture Magazine

PHOTOPLAY

April

The
Studio
Secret

The
Tragedies
of Pauline
Frederick

VALENTINO'S HOLLYWOOD LIFE

A BREWSTER PUBLICATION

Motion Picture.

MAY

MAGAZINE

25

Gloria Swanson

Humphrey Bogart (1900–1957) was a star in his life-time; after his death he became a cult. Whatever his role, he was always Bogart, tough, cynical, heroic and a loner. He was one of the screen's best gangsters. He regarded acting as a job, always gave an honest performance, and off-screen was as liked and respected as a man as he was as an actor. After many fine roles supporting such stars as Cagney and Edward G. Robinson, he established himself in the front rank as a private eye in *The Maltese Falcon* (1942). Other memorable roles were as a bar proprietor in *Casablanca* (1942); with Lauren Bacall in *To Have and Have Not* (1944), from which the still is taken, *The Big Sleep* (1946) and *Key Largo* (1948); *The Treasure of Sierra Madre* (1948); as a drunken soft-hearted owner of the boat *The African Queen* (1951); and as the paranoic Captain Queeg in *The Caine Mutiny* (1954).

Lauren Bacall (1924–   ) made her first film, *To Have and Have Not* (1944), opposite Bogart, whom she tells to whistle if he wants anything. Their acting suggested a mutual sympathy, and their marriage and obvious happiness brought satisfaction to many in the film industry. Her best films were those she made with Bogart in the next three or four years – apart from *How to Marry a Millionaire* (1953) her subsequent films were not as good as she deserved. Her screen personality is best described as sexy. Like Bogart, she suggested toughness, independence and hidden depths. None was better at weighing up a man and implying that she expected him to reciprocate. Her most recent successes have been on the stage.

Clark Gable (1901–1960) was the king of modern romantic leads, handsome, virile and manly. He also had a casual rakish air which appealed to women. He was thirty before he got a decent part, and then several films made in a year or two began his rise to stardom. *It Happened One Night* (1934) and *Mutiny on the Bounty* (1935) took him right to the top. In 1940 came the role by which he is best remembered, as Rhett Butler in *Gone With the Wind* (1939), one of the biggest financial successes of all time. No future role could match this, but in his last film, *The Misfits* (1961), completed just before he died, he could still show the quality which made him a star – uncomplicated masculinity.

Joan Crawford (1904–), seen here with Gable in *Strange Cargo* (1940), is undoubtedly a star. She is hardly anything else, and anybody attempting to define stardom might do well to look at Joan Crawford's career. She began in 1925, as a flapper-cum-dancer, but there have been better dancers. She has played romantic leads, but there have been more attractive actresses. She has been in comedy, but is no comedienne, and has played heavy roles in melodramas, but is not a great actress. But she has always projected the image of a star: choosing her roles, insisting on the best billing, even counting her fan letters, and it must be admitted that however mediocre her films (and most of them are) audiences have consistently turned up to see her for fifty years. Perhaps survival is the main ingredient of stardom.

Cary Grant (1904–) played Cary Grant in films for over thirty years. His assets were a dimple in his chin, an odd hair-style, a handsome face never quite in or out of fashion, a capacity for never growing a day older, an amusing quizzical expression, an easy charm, an elegant figure, a casual grace in movement and a nice sense of comedy timing. He needed no more, and audiences expected no more. His leading ladies included Mae West, Jean Harlow, Katharine Hepburn, Ingrid Bergman, and Audrey Hepburn. His directors included Hitchcock (many times), Cukor, Capra, Hawks and Kramer. He has mixed with the best, and they haven't changed him a bit: his urbanity remains unruffled.

Katharine Hepburn (1909–), seen here with Grant in *Holiday* (1940), had a very individual charm. She was not beautiful, has always had her share of detractors and has even been labelled 'box-office poison', yet she grew on audiences and eventually was indisputably a star. It was of her that Dorothy Parker said: 'She ran the gamut of emotions from A to B', but others have called her a great actress. She was at her best in sophisticated comedy like *Bringing Up Baby* (1938), *The Philadelphia Story* (1940), and the ten films with Spencer Tracy, with whom it is thought she was in love. *The African Queen* (1951) was a *tour de force*, and *The Lion in Winter* (1968) won her a third Oscar 35 years after her first.

NINOTCHKA
with Greta GARBO

"I love you, Ninotchka... it's the one serious thing in my life!"

Gloria Swanson (1898–   ) was *the* great lady of the silents. She was glamorous, she was sophisticated, and her clothes and her second marriage (to a real live French marquis) were a fan's delight. *That* career began in earnest when she went to Paramount to work for DeMille in films like *Don't Change Your Husband* (1919), *Male and Female* (1919) and *The Affairs of Anatol* (1921), quite a change from the Mack Sennett shorts in which she'd revealed a talent for comedy. Romance followed romance, filmically speaking, and all the time she was pushing her star status. By 1923 she was choosing her vehicles more carefully, and in 1926 she began producing herself. *Sadie Thompson* (1928) and *The Trespasser* (1929) did well but after that it was all downhill. Since 1941 she's been staging comebacks, but the greatest was undoubtedly *Sunset Boulevard* (1950).

Melvyn Douglas (1901–   ) spent much of his early movie career playing a sort of second-string William Powell. He was always polished, suave and witty, playing leading man to many of the great ladies of Hollywood in the 1930s and 1940s, but never quite achieving the stature of Powell — until the latter fell ill and Douglas stepped into his shoes opposite Garbo in *Ninotchka* (1939). It was his second film with Garbo, the first being *As You Desire Me* (1932), and was a great success for them both. Douglas forsook Hollywood for Broadway in the late 1940s, where he pursued a much more productive and satisfying career as an actor. When he returned to Hollywood it was as a character actor playing Dansker in *Billy Bud* (1962). His performance as the grandfather in *Hud* the following year won him a Best Supporting Actor Oscar.

Greta Garbo (1905–   ) is the one
star on whom the Hollywood
superlatives sit lightly. She was, she is
still, the one true goddess of the screen.
Many miles of prose have been devoted
to the attempt to define her talent and
words like 'mystery' and 'enigma' tend
to crop up a lot. And rightly so perhaps.
Those the camera loves, it reveals. All,
that is, but Garbo. Her first Hollywood
film, *The Torrent* (1926), was an
enormous hit, and amongst her other
silents the three made with John Gilbert
did particularly well, her greatest
subsequent roles being *Queen Christina*
(1933) and *Camille* (1936). In 1939
MGM tried her in comedy; *Ninotchka*
was good but *Two-Faced Woman*
(1941) was disastrous and she has done
nothing since. Here she is in *The Kiss*
(1930), her last silent.

Marlene Dietrich (1901–   ) is the
screen's greatest femme fatale. Furred
and feathered or dressed down in male
drag, she challenged every man she met
while lightly, wittily sending up the
whole pantomime. She'd been in films
and theatre for about twelve years when
von Sternberg chose her for *The Blue
Angel* (1930), and she went to
Hollywood to do his *Morocco* (1930),
staying to make others with him,
including *Shanghai Express* (1932) and
The Devil is a Woman (1935). The best
things of the next few years were
Borzage's *Desire* (1936), Lubitsch's
Angel (1937) and the comedy *Destry
Rides Again* (1939, seen here). Most of
her later material was weak, welcome
exceptions being Wilder's *A Foreign
Affair* (1948) and Lang's *Rancho
Notorious* (1952). Since 1961 she has
pursued a singing career, appearing in
theatres and cabaret all over the world.

HD-46

Bette Davis (1908–) is one of the screen's greatest actresses, which is what she always meant to be. She had something a lot rarer than good looks – an intense, powerful acting style compounded of equal parts of intelligence and emotion – and she fought to use it. *Of Human Bondage* (1934) was her first big chance and more goodies followed, including *Dangerous* (1935, seen here) and *The Petrified Forest* (1936), but it was hard work persuading Warners what sort of material she'd accept. She tried, unsuccessfully, to renege on her contract and after that they took the hint, with films like *Jezebel* (1938), *Dark Victory* (1939), *The Private Lives of Elizabeth and Essex* (1939) and *The Little Foxes* (1941). Since 1946 her luck's been much less even, though *All About Eve* (1950), *Whatever Happened to Baby Jane?* (1962) and *Hush Hush Sweet Charlotte* (1965) were all high spots.

Elizabeth Taylor (1932–　) was a very big star in the 1960s. That she was may say more about the public's appetite for sensationalism than it does about her talent. By the age of eleven she was under contract to MGM, the best thing she did as a child being *National Velvet* (1944). They let her grow up, but nothing much clicked apart from *A Place in the Sun* (1951), *Giant* (1956), and *Raintree Country* (1957). With her private life hitting the headlines she did a trio of popular sexy dramas, *Cat on a Hot Tin Roof* (1958), *Suddenly Last Summer* (1959), and *Butterfield 8* (1960). Next came *Cleopatra* (1963), of which least said . . ., and a string of movies with husband Richard Burton. Some were fairly awful, among them *The Sandpiper* (1965, seen here), but *Who's Afraid of Virginia Woolf?* (1966) and *The Taming of the Shrew* (1967) were really very good.

Rita Hayworth (1918–　) began her show-business career at the tender age of six in her father's troupe, The Dancing Cansinos. By the 1930s, she was playing in Westerns and B features under her own name, Margarita (later Rita) Cansino. A seven-year contract with Columbia in 1937 really got her career moving. They changed her name to Hayworth and helped her develop the image — a combination of auburn-haired charm and erotic glamour — which made her a favourite pin-up of the Second World War and one of the screen's best remembered Love Goddesses. Not much of a singer, she danced marvellously with Fred Astaire in *You'll Never Get Rich* (1941) and *You Were Never Lovelier* (1942) and with Gene Kelly in *Cover Girl* (1944). Other splendid Hayworth performances were in *Blood and Sand* (1941), *Gilda* (1946), *Miss Sadie Thompson* (1953), *Pal Joey* (1957) and *Separate Tables* (1958).

Sophia Loren (1934—   ) is warm and generous and beautiful. She broke into films about 1950 and soon met Carlo Ponti (whom she married in 1957). Come 1955 he'd begun to build her internationally in films like *L'Ora di Napoli* and *La Donna del Fiume*. The American series she made between 1957 and 1960, films like *Boy on a Dolphin* (1957, seen here) and *Desire Under the Elms* (1958), were a disappointment. Her greatest international success has been in the Italian *Two Women* (1961) but she was also popular in *Boccaccio '70* (1962), *Yesterday, Today and Tomorrow* (1964) and *Marriage Italian Style* (1964). The second American series, with films like *Lady L* (1965) and *A Countess from Hong Kong* (1967), did no better than the first, and since 1970 her films have had more success in the Italian market than internationally.

201

Rudolph Valentino (1895–1926) tango-ed his way to movie stardom in *The Four Horsemen of the Apocalypse* (1921), in which he is shown (*right*) with Alice Terry, actress wife of the film's director, Rex Ingram. By the time he had exchanged his Latin American gear of *Four Horsemen* for the burnous and turban of *The Sheik* (1921), Valentino was – as far as women movie fans were concerned, anyway – the world's Number One screen idol. His acting style and techniques were minimal, but he had a magnetic sexuality which, when shown at its best in films like *Blood and Sand* (1922) and *The Son of the Sheik* (1925), more than compensated. He died of a perforated ulcer in 1926; the funeral almost brought New York to a standstill.

Gary Cooper (1901–1961) made more than ninety movies in his thirty-five years in the business, and in most of them he was a star – one of Hollywood's genuine, enduring all-time Greats. He usually appeared as the quietly determined and courageous good man, as in both the films for which he won Oscars, *Sergeant York* (1941) and *High Noon* (1952). Some of his best films were Westerns, including *The Virginian* (1929), his first big talkie, *The Plainsman* (1936) and, of course, *High Noon*, but he was by no means solely a Western star. One of his best-remembered films is the Capra comedy *Mr Deeds Goes to Town* (1936). Other good ones were *A Farewell to Arms* (1932), *Lives of a Bengal Lancer* (1935) and *Vera Cruz* (1954). The still shows him in *Saratoga Trunk* (1945) with Ingrid Bergman.

Ingrid Bergman (1915–) was a film star in Sweden before she followed in Garbo's footsteps to Hollywood in 1938, and American audiences soon warmed to her fresh naturalness and charm. When she teamed up with Bogart in *Casablanca* (1942) and with Cooper in *For Whom the Bell Tolls* (1943), she was well on the way to being queen of Hollywood, a position in no way imperilled by the success of films like *Gaslight* (1944), for which she won an Oscar, *Spellbound* and *The Bells of St Mary's* (1945), and *Notorious* (1946). She became notorious herself for her affair with Italian director Roberto Rossellini, which halted her American career in its tracks. She came back ten years later with *Anastasia* (1957) and a second Oscar.

Vivien Leigh (1913–1967) was the breathtakingly lovely English actress who walked off with the plum actress's part of all time when she was cast as Scarlett O'Hara in *Gone With the Wind* (1939). She was virtually unknown in Hollywood, but an Oscar for *Gone With the Wind* changed all that. Even so she was better known as a personality and a stage actress than as a film star, and had to wait twelve years for her next really good film role. It was Blanche in *A Streetcar Named Desire* (1951), and her interpretation of the Tennessee Williams' character won her another Oscar. Her other films included *Fire Over England* (1937) and *That Hamilton Woman* (1941), both with her husband, Laurence Olivier, Gabriel Pascal's *Caesar and Cleopatra* (1945), Korda's *Anna Karenina* (1948), *The Deep Blue Sea* (1956), *The Roman Spring of Mrs Stone* (1961) and *Ship of Fools* (1965).

Marlon Brando (1924–   ) is a superb actor who has also been one of America's leading – though notoriously 'difficult' – film stars for twenty-five years. He acted successfully on Broadway for some years before making his first film, *The Men*, in 1950. His performance as Stanley Kowalski in *A Streetcar Named Desire* had been a Broadway success which he repeated to great critical acclaim in the 1951 film version. *Viva Zapata!* (1952), *The Wild One* and *On the Waterfront* (1954) added to his reputation, but many of his later films received mixed praise and censure, the latter generally for the films rather than his performances in them. Just when people were beginning to write off his career, he came back with two smash hits, *The Godfather*, for which he won an Oscar, and *Last Tango in Paris* (1972). The photograph shows Leigh and Brando in *A Streetcar Named Desire*.

Steve McQueen (1932–) is his own man. The image is casual, independent; no one ever puts anything across him. It's no surprise then to find him among the superstars of the pragmatic 1970s. He began in the theatre and started picking up a lot of TV work after a stage success in 1956. There were some important parts in unimportant films and then Sinatra offered him the big break, *Never So Few* (1958), and that won him the third lead in *The Magnificent Seven* (1960). Since then there've been three well-spaced good parts in three popular well-made movies – *The Great Escape* (1963), *The Cincinnati Kid* (1965, seen here), and *Bullitt* (1969). The fans seemed to like him in most of the rest too, films like *Nevada Smith* (1966), *The Thomas Crown Affair* (1968), *Junior Bonner* (1972), and *Getaway* (1972).

Jack Nicholson (1937–) is that rare breed a star and an actor: most of those who've made it in the movies have gotten on by being either one or the other. That his charm is considerable is obvious, though his voice is slow, almost monotonal, and of his talent there's been no doubt since *Easy Rider* (1969). He'd been around for eleven years when that film was made, mostly in cheap, fringe Hollywood productions, acting, co-producing, and writing. The next, a musical in 1970 with Barbra Streisand, was a mistake, but since then he's given a series of excellent and varied performances in mostly good movies, among them *Five Easy Pieces* (1970, seen here), *Carnal Knowledge* (1971), *The King of Marvin Gardens* (1972), *The Last Detail* (1973) and *Chinatown* (1974). In 1970 he also directed *Drive He Said*.

Charlton Heston (1923–) was Hollywood's very own homo epicus. His shoulders were broad, his gaze was direct, and he stood very tall. He might be boring, but he always looked good. Cecil B. DeMille, who knew about these things, saw it first and put him into *The Ten Commandments* (1956) as Moses, rescuing him from an almost unbroken line of B features. Only his Mark Antony in *Julius Caesar* (1948) and the lead in DeMille's *The Greatest Show on Earth* (1952) had been of much account. More heroics followed, both ancient and modern: *The Buccaneer* (1958), *Ben Hur* (1959, seen here), *El Cid* (1961), *The Greatest Story Ever Told* (1965), *The Agony and the Ecstasy* (1965), *The War Lord* (1965), *Khartoum* (1966), and *Antony and Cleopatra* (1972), which he also scripted and directed. Away from the spectacle, he turned in some competent performances in *Touch of Evil* (1957) and *Major Dundee* (1965).

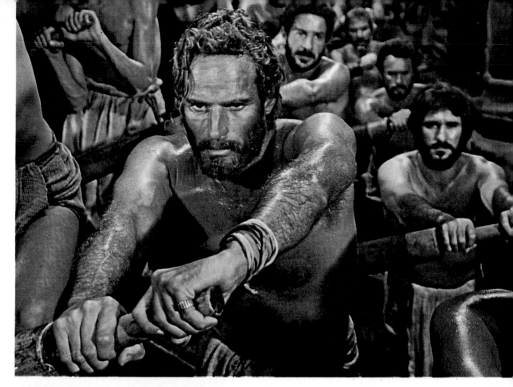

Errol Flynn (1909–1959) was a rousing, rollicking boyo. In Jack Warner's famous words '. . . he showered an audience with sparks when he laughed, when he fought, or when he loved.' See him in *The Sea Hawk* (1940) and you get the general idea. Teamed with the gentle, ladylike Olivia de Havilland, Warner Brothers had an unbeatable property. *Captain Blood* (1935), *The Charge of the Light Brigade* (1936), *The Adventures of Robin Hood* (1938), and *They Died with Their Boots On* (1941) – these rank with the most memorable action-romances of all time. After de Havilland grew bored and left, after the scandal began breaking, he was never again so good. His style of swashbuckling couldn't be grafted on to the war movie without offence, and only *The Adventures of Don Juan* (1948) had him back to something like his old form. There were, however, three good (though in light of the facts, sad) performances as a drunk. Here he is in *Dodge City* (1939).

The Hollywood Studios

Hollywood became more than the centre of film-making: Hollywood *meant* films, and its name will always be associated with the golden age of the industry.

In 1908, the film industry was centred in New York, where several leading American and French companies formed the Motion Pictures Patent Company, designed to gain a world monopoly in the production, distribution and exhibition of films. Bitter legal (and often illegal) battles ensued and forced independent producers and exhibitors to move away, and the Hollywood district of Los Angeles, together with its neighbouring Beverly Hills, Bel-Air and San Fernando Valley, became their headquarters.

The major studios whose names and trade marks became world famous were: Universal (the spinning globe), Twentieth Century-Fox (its name like a building illuminated with searchlights), Paramount (a mountain wreathed in stars), United Artists (a plain lozenge), Warner Brothers (WB in a shield), MGM (the roaring lion) and Columbia (the Statue of Liberty). The moguls who set up and ruled these companies were often cinema-owning European immigrants who saw production and distribution as a logical extension of their activities.

Carl Laemmle began with a Chicago nickelodeon, formed Universal and opened his studio, Universal City, in San Fernando Valley in 1915. William Fox, once a clothier, began production with the Fox Film Corporation in 1915. This became Twentieth Century-Fox in 1935 when Darryl F. Zanuck and Joseph Schenk merged it with their Twentieth Century Picture Storporation.

Adolph Zukor, once a furrier, defied the Patents Company and imported

left
Irving Thalberg (*left*) and Louis B. Mayer with Mary Pickford in 1925, soon after the formation of MGM.

above
Walter Greene presenting a book of signatures to Adolf Zukor (*centre*) and Jesse Lasky (*right*) about 1919.

Queen Elizabeth, starring Sarah Bernhardt. Its success encouraged him to begin producing in 1913. His company, Famous Players in Famous Plays, joined Jesse Lasky Feature Plays, founded the same year, to become Famous Players-Lasky in 1916. Lasky had formed his company with his brother-in-law Samuel Goldfisch (later Goldwyn) and Cecil B. DeMille. Goldwyn was in many ways the most interesting of the Hollywood moguls. From the 1920s he produced independently, financing his own productions. His astuteness and success were overshadowed by his philistinism, which manifested itself in those curious phrases of mangled English known as Goldwynisms, such as (of a book) 'I read part of it all the way through.' The Famous Players-Lasky films were distributed by Paramount, which was acquired in 1917 and eventually became the name of the whole company, headed by Zukor.

United Artists was formed in 1919 by D. W. Griffith, Charles Chaplin, Mary Pickford and Douglas Fairbanks to use their combined talents, but Griffith soon left and Chaplin made only seven films for the company.

David O. Selznick signing Vivien Leigh for the part of Scarlett O'Hara in *Gone With the Wind* (1939). Two other stars of the picture, Leslie Howard and Olivia de Havilland, watch.

Independent producer Sam Goldwyn and his wife. Despite the Goldwynism 'Include me out', he cannot be omitted from a gallery of movie moguls.

The Warner brothers, Harry, Albert, Sam and Jack, sold soap, meat and ice-cream before becoming film exhibitors and distributors. They bought two old production companies, Vitagraph and First National, to form Warner Brothers in 1923. In the 1960s the company was taken over by Seven Arts and became Warner-7 Arts.

MGM was a triple merger designed by Marcus Loew, of the widespread theatre chain, Loew's Inc., to produce films. He first bought the Metro company and later the Mayer Studio and the Goldwyn Picture Corporation (Goldwyn left before the merger). Louis B. Mayer became production head of the new Metro-Goldwyn-

Mayer on its formation in 1924 and remained so till 1951. The 25-year-old Irving Thalberg, previously a protégé of Carl Laemmle at Universal, became Mayer's second-in-command. His meteoric rise made him a legend among producers, and he was the model for Monroe Stahr in Scott Fitzgerald's 'The Last Tycoon'.

Columbia, formed in 1924, grew out of the CBC Company of Joe Brandt and Jack and Harry Cohn, who was head of production till his death in 1958. Once a bus conductor, he was brought into films by Carl Laemmle.

The studios are often criticized for their commercialism, leading to the

left
Carl Laemmle, senior and junior, in the
Universal City studios.

below
Darryl F. Zanuck in the Paris studios
making *The Longest Day* (1962).

emphasis on the star system, and
regarded as the enemy of art, but the
fact remains that many of the great
films were products of the studio
system. The way *Gone With the Wind*
was casted might be sneered at, but
David O. Selznick, the producer,
could point to an end-product which
gave pleasure to millions. The studios
developed identities: Warners were
at the forefront of technical innovations, and made many of the great
gangster films with Edward G. Robinson and Humphrey Bogart. Fox
specialized in blondes, from Betty
Grable to Marilyn Monroe. Universal,
under Laemmle, imported the great
German directors and led the horror
movement with Frankenstein and
Dracula. Paramount made great comedies with Fields, the Marx Brothers,
Mae West, Hope and Crosby, not to
mention Lubitsch. MGM made the
best musicals, and brought Garbo to
Hollywood.

The power of the studios was
largely broken in 1948, when Anti-
Trust Laws forced them to divorce
cinema ownership from production
and distribution. In the late 1960s
many made huge losses in the face of
television competition, and they are
now part of conglomerate companies
dealing in real estate and other prosaic
commodities. However, they remain
the major force in film-making, still
responsible for the greater share of the
box office takings of the world.

Awards and Festivals

Among the methods of publicizing films are film festivals and the giving of awards. Festivals are a pleasant way of advertising a particular country's film industry. Critics come from other countries to see both the local product and the foreign films, often shown before their general release, and a distinguished jury makes awards. Usually there are attendant exhibitions and seminars, and the presence of stars ensures good publicity. In the days of ambitious starlets, the publicity was not always good, as on the occasion when a young lady was photographed topless in the sea, for the delectation and censure of the world's newspaper readers. The distinguished Venice Film Festival was begun in 1932, and the very successful Cannes Festival in 1946 (Brigitte Bardot was discovered there in 1953). America has five annual festivals, and there is now hardly a film-producing country without its festival.

The most famous award in the film business is the Oscar. Since 1927, when the Academy Awards, as they are properly called, were instituted, several have been awarded in various categories annually. They are the results of ballots among the members of the Academy of Motion Picture Arts and Sciences, and the most sought-after are those for the Actor and Actress of the Year. Garbo didn't win one, but Joan Crawford and Bette Davis did. Olivier, Bogart and Brando all won Oscars. The Academy Awards do not necessarily go to the best, and George C. Scott, an outspoken critic of the system, refused to accept his in 1970, but they provide drama, discussion and publicity each year.

Oscar ceremony: Spencer Tracy (Best Actor for *Boys' Town*) and Bette Davis (Best Actress for *Jezebel*) with their 1938 Oscars. Miss Davis is receiving hers from Cedric Hardwicke.

West Side Story won ten Oscars in 1961, including Best Picture. George Chakiris (*left*), leader of the Sharks, was Best Supporting Actor. He is facing Russ Tamblyn, leader of the Jets.

Colour, Sound and the

Colour was an early pre-occupation with film-makers, and hand colouring of films began almost at once. A process known as Kinemacolor was patented by G. A. Smith in 1906 and used red and green filters in photography to produce a coloured effect when projected. Experiments by Technicolor Inc, the most famous name in film colour, led to a three-colour process for Disney's *Flowers and Trees* in 1932. The system was widely used till the 1950s when Eastman Colour refined it further.

The film associated with the coming of sound is *The Jazz Singer* (1927), but sound on disc had accompanied film since 1896, and the Fox Movietone News filmed famous men talking in April 1927. *The Jazz Singer* appeared in October with talking and singing sequences. The first all-talking picture was *The Lights of New York* (1928).

The making of wide-screen pictures was a desperate measure to stop falling attendances in the 1950s. The use of three projectors to show films on three overlapping screens was used by Abel Gance, in four sequences of his film

left
Warner Brothers making the most of a 'supreme triumph'. The film which meant death to the silents, *The Jazz Singer* (1927) 'as produced on the spoken stage'.

top right
Wide screen, 1927. Abel Gance used three screens and projectors for *Napoléon*, sometimes to make a single picture, sometimes for three separate pictures, and sometimes to repeat a single picture three times. This still shows one picture spread across three screens.

right
Helen Costello in the first all-talking feature film, the musical *Lights of New York* (1928).

Wide Screen

above
A battle scene from the Cinerama production *Battle of the Bulge* (1965) in Ultra-Panavision and Technicolor.

right
The first CinemaScope feature, *The Robe* (1953). Richard Burton addressing Jean Simmons and Jay Robinson.

Napoléon (1927). The idea was revived, and *This is Cinerama*, an exhibition film, was shown in 1952. The first conventional feature of the revival was *How the West Was Won* (1962). CinemaScope, a wide-screen system using an anamorphic lens, which squeezes a wide image into a standard frame, was first used in *The Robe* (1953), although it, too, was invented years earlier. Norman McLaren made a film *Around is Around* (1951), with a three-dimensional effect (again an old idea) and in 1953 *Bwana Devil* was the first of a commercial string of such pictures. Special spectacles were needed for viewing – a nuisance which killed the idea. A 3D system without the need for spectacles has been developed in Russia by Semyon Ivanov, but has not yet reached the West.

The Cinema Now

The Civil Rights movement in America was reflected in the increased importance of the roles given black actors in the movies. Diana Ross' superb performance as the singer Billie Holiday in *Lady Sings the Blues* (1972) was nominated for an Oscar.

The cinema has seen many changes in the past ten years or so – probably more than at any time in its eighty-year history. Television has been responsible for some of the changes. The people who used to go to the pictures regularly every week, seeing whatever was showing, now sit at home in front of the television screen. Cinema attendances began dropping in the 1950s, and kept on falling in every country where television operated on a big scale. By the 1970s, the cinema was no longer the major mass medium. Indeed, it was hardly a mass medium at all, having to appeal now to a series of minority audiences, ranging from the devotees of gothic horror at one end of the spectrum to the followers of foreign films, the avant-garde and the underground film at the other.

The enormous cost involved in making films has been another cause of changes in the cinema industry. The studio system, and the stars system it created and supported, have both disappeared. The props on the Metro-Goldwyn-Mayer lot were sold in 1970, those at Twentieth Century-Fox in 1971.

If the cinema industry has changed, so too has the style of the films being made in the 1970s. Throughout the Western world, the 1960s saw a marked relaxation in standards of social behaviour, both private and public, and, consequently, in the rules of censorship. The cinema, partly in an attempt to win back its audiences, was well in the front in this movement. By the end of the 1960s, it was showing explicit and uninhibited sex scenes as a matter of course in major feature films. The naked wrestling bout between Oliver Reed and Alan Bates in Ken Russell's *Women in Love* (1969) was different enough at the time to cause a stir, although the scene in the same film in which Glenda Jackson appeared naked in bed with Oliver Reed passed without comment.

By the beginning of the 1970s, when sex in all its aspects – lesbian, as in *The Killing of Sister George* (1968), homosexual as in *Sunday, Bloody Sunday* (1971), prostituted as in *Klute* (1971), or Andy Warhol's *Flesh* (1968) – had become acceptable as an adult, serious subject for discussion in films, and was anyway losing 'commercial' ground to the pornography and 'blue movie' merchants, the cinema turned to violence and gore. Sam Peckinpah's *The Wild Bunch* (1969) and *Straw Dogs* (1971) were both criticized for their violence, particularly the latter. The sadistic violence of much of

Richard Roundtree as Harlem private detective *Shaft* (1971). The black movie became a major force in the American cinema from the late 1960s, and Richard Roundtree was one of several actors, including Jim Brown and Paul Winfield, who began challenging Sidney Poitier's and Harry Belafonte's lonely eminence as the U.S.'s major black actors.

left
Twiggy in Ken Russell's sparkling
re-creation of the world of Busby
Berkeley, *The Boyfriend* (1971).

top
Alan Bates and Oliver Reed wrestle
naked in Ken Russell's *Women in Love*
(1969).

above
Brenda Vaccaro and Jon Voight in
Midnight Cowboy (1969).

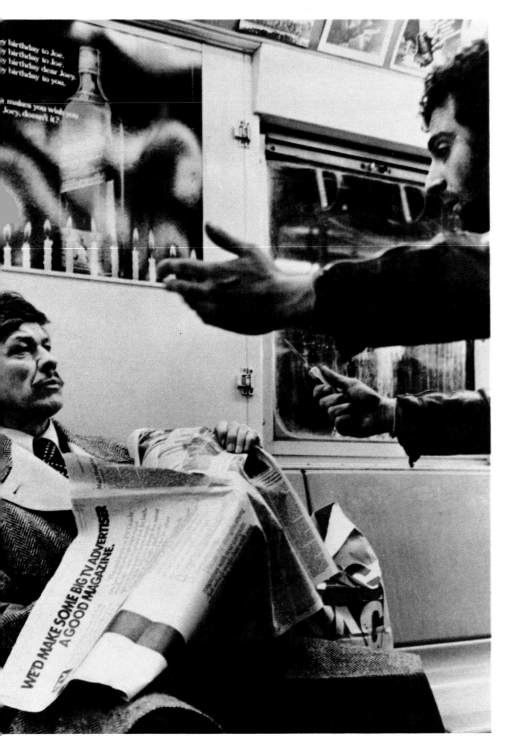

Stanley Kubrick's brilliant *A Clockwork Orange* (1971) led to many dis-
cussions in the media as to whether
violence on the screen could be an
evil influence in real life. One of the
most commercially successful films of
1974/5 was Michael Winner's *Death
Wish*, in which Charles Bronson,
seeking to avenge the murder of his
wife and the rape of his daughter at
the hands of a gang of psychopaths
who break into his apartment, takes
the law into his own hands, killing
muggers and other criminals he encounters in the streets. To his neigh-
bours, beleaguered in the violent streets
of the modern city, he becomes a
hero, a figure to emulate. It was a

particularly violent re-application of the ethics of the Western.

Another genre finding itself re-worked in the 1970s has been the epic. This time the block-buster has moved from Ancient Rome and the Second World War to the sort of disaster which might afflict modern society. *The Poseidon Adventure* had an ocean liner turned upside-down by a tidal wave. The ship in *Juggernaut* was loaded to its plimsoll line with bombs. When *Earthquake* hit the screen, the very cinema seats rocked under the influence of Sensurround. It took the combined resources of two film companies, Warners and Twentieth Century-Fox, to bring the modern

city-dwellers' nightmare to the screen: *The Towering Inferno* had a glittering party of film stars trapped on the 138th floor of the world's tallest building while a fire started on the 81st floor raged closer.

If films like these disaster epics, or like *Death Wish*, *Serpico* and *The Exorcist*, with their underlying scepti-cism about the effectiveness of the forces of law and order in society, show a disillusion with modern life, then the retreat into nostalgia and the past (even if it is a violent one), which has been a major feature of the 1970s cinema, is all the more understandable.

The Summer of '42 was followed by *The Class of '44* (1974). *The Way We*

Disaster was a theme of many 1970s box-office successes. *The Towering Inferno* (1975) had all the right epic ingredients, including a large cast, splendid sets and fearful drama.

Were went back to the 1940s, and *Badlands* (1974) to the pulp magazine world of the 1950s. Peter Bogdanovich, whose *The Last Picture Show* (1971) showed the decay of a Western town in the 1950s, went back to the 1930s Depression in his Oscar-winning *Paper Moon* (1973). Paul Newman and Robert Redford, having been a hugely successful partnership in *Butch Cassidy and the Sundance Kid*, teamed up again in the 1920s for *The Sting* (1973), music by courtesy of nostalgic Scott Joplin.

The cinema's most evocative nostalgia trip of the early 1970s was MGM's reliving of its best musical moments in *That's Entertainment* (1974). When Fred Astaire and Eleanor Powell finished their tap-dance routine, cinema audiences cheered, then sighed 'They don't make them like that anymore'. They will probably be saying the same thing of the 1970s' films in the 1990s. For, even if the cinema changes and changes again, films will still be made, for the moving picture is the twentieth century's main form of communication, and its own art form.

left
Julie Christie in Joseph Losey's
The Go-Between (1971).

below left
Robert Shaw, Robert Redford and Paul
Newman in *The Sting* (1973).

below
Ryan and Tatum O'Neal in Peter
Bogdanovich's *Paper Moon* (1973).

Acknowledgments

The authors and publisher acknowledge with thanks the help of the following people, organizations, film companies, and distributors in the provision of the illustrations for this book:
ABC, AFE Corporation, Allied Artists, Angel Films, Associated British, Astor Pictures, BFI/BBC, British Lion, Kevin Brownlow, Chartoff-Winkler, Cinerama, Carlos Clarens, Columbia, Contemporary Films, Continental, Bill Douglas, Ealing Studios, Film Polski, First National, Gainsborough, Gaumont, Gaumont British, Goldwyn, Halas and Batchelor, Hammer Films, Hungarofilm, ICAIC, Janus Films, Keystone, King Features – Subafilms, London, Mayer-Burstyn, Metro, MGM, MGM-EMI, Miracle Films, Nero Films, Paramount (CIC), Pathé, Rank Film Distributors, Riama-Film, RKO Radio, Royal Films International, Sandrews, Selznick, Staatl Filmarchiv der DDR, Twentieth Century-Fox, United Artists, Universal, Universal International, UFA, Walt Disney, Warner Brothers, Warner Brothers– First National, Warner Brothers– Seven Arts, Zagreb Film.

Picture Research by JOHN KOBAL

Bibliography

Among the many books the authors found helpful, they particularly recommend the following:
The American Movies by Paul Michael (editor-in-chief). Garland Books, New York, 1969.
Antonioni by Ian Cameron and Robin Wood. Studio Vista, London, 1970 (2nd edition).
Buster Keaton by David Robinson. Secker & Warburg, London, 1969.
The Cinema of Fritz Lang by Paul M. Jensen. A. S. Barnes, New York, and A. Zwemmer, London, 1969.
The Cinema of John Ford by John Baxter. A. S. Barnes, New York, and A. Zwemmer, London, 1971.
The Crazy Mirror by Raymond Durgnat. Faber and Faber, London, 1969.
Documentary Diary by Paul Rotha. Secker & Warburg, London, 1973.
Film Censors and the Law by Neville March Hunnings. Allen & Unwin, London, 1967.
The Filmgoer's Companion by Leslie Halliwell. MacGibbon & Kee, London, 1967 (second edition).
Films in America 1929–1969 by Martin Quigley Jr and Richard Gertner. Golden Press, New York, 1970
The Films of Laurel and Hardy by William K. Everson. Citadel Press, New York, 1967.
The Film Till Now by Paul Rotha. Spring Books, London, 1967.
Focus on Hitchcock edited by Albert J. LaValley. Prentice-Hall, New Jersey, 1972.
The Great British Picture Show by George Perry. Hart-Davis, MacGibbon, London, 1974.
The Great Movies by William Bayer. Hamlyn, London, 1973.
The Great Movie Stars: The Golden Years by David Shipman. Hamlyn, London, 1970.
The Great Movie Stars: The International Years by David Shipman. Angus & Robertson, London, 1972.
Hollywood and After by Jerzy Toeplitz. Allen & Unwin, London, 1974.
Hollywood in the Thirties by John Baxter. Zwemmer, London, and A. S. Barnes, New York, 1968.
Hollywood in the Twenties by David Robinson. Zwemmer, London, and A. S. Barnes, New York, 1968.
The Hollywood Musical by John Russell Taylor and Arthur Jackson. Secker & Warburg, London, 1971.
Horror in the Cinema by Ivan Butler. Zwemmer, London, and A. S. Barnes, New York, 1970.
Horror Movies: An Illustrated Survey by Carlos Clarens. Secker & Warburg, London, 1968.
Howard Hawks edited by Joseph McBride. Prentice-Hall, New Jersey, 1972.
The International Encyclopedia of Film edited by Dr Roger Manvell. Michael Joseph, London, 1972.
Mack Sennett's Keystone by Kalton C. Lahue. A. S. Barnes, New York, and Thomas Yoseloff, London, 1971.
Movie Moguls by Philip French. Weidenfeld and Nicolson, London, 1969.
The Movies by Richard Griffith and Arthur Mayer. Spring Books, London, 1971 (second edition).
The Musical Film by Douglas McVay. Barnes, New York, and Zwemmer, London, 1967.
New Cinema in Eastern Europe by Alistair Whyte. Studio Vista, London, 1971.
Orson Welles by Joseph McBride. Secker & Warburg, London, 1972.
The Parade's Gone By by Kevin Brownlow. Secker & Warburg, London, 1968.
A Pictorial History of Crime Films by Ian Cameron. Hamlyn, London, 1975.
A Pictorial History of Film Musicals by John Kobal. Hamlyn, London, 1970.
A Pictorial History of Horror Movies by Denis Gifford. Hamlyn, London, 1973.
A Pictorial History of Sex in the Movies by Jeremy Pascall and Clyde Jeavons. Hamlyn, London, 1975.
A Pictorial History of the Silent Screen by Daniel Blum. Spring Books, London, 1962.
A Pictorial History of the Talkies by Daniel Blum. Spring Books, London, 1974 (second revised edition).
A Pictorial History of the Western Film by William K. Everson. Citadel Press, New York, 1969.
A Pictorial History of War Films by Clyde Jeavons. Hamlyn, London, 1974.
A Pictorial History of Westerns by Michael Parkinson and Clyde Jeavons. Hamlyn, London, 1972.
The Rise of the American Film by Lewis Jacobs. Teachers College Press, New York, 1939.
Romance and the Cinema by John Kobal. Studio Vista, London, 1973.
The Silent Cinema by Liam O'Leary. Studio Vista, London/Dutton, New York, 1965.
Spectacular! by John Cary and John Kobal. Hamlyn, London, 1974.
Stanley Kubrick Directs by Alexander Walker. Davis-Poynter, London, 1972.
Westerns by Philip French. Secker & Warburg/British Film Institute, London, 1973.
What the Censor Saw by John Trevelyan. Michael Joseph, London, 1973.
World Cinema by David Robinson. Eyre Methuen, London, 1973.